SCENES FROM EURIPIDES'
TROJAN WOMEN

RUINS OF THE THEATRE AT EPIDAUROS

SCENES FROM EURIPIDES'

TROJAN WOMEN

EDITED WITH AN INTRODUCTION, NOTES
AND VOCABULARY

BY

F. KINCHIN SMITH, M.A.(Oxon)

LATE SENIOR LECTURER IN CLASSICS
UNIVERSITY OF LONDON INSTITUTE OF EDUCATION

AND

BARBARA J. HODGE, M.A. (Cantab)

LECTURER IN CLASSICS
UNIVERSITY OF LONDON INSTITUTE OF EDUCATION

LONDON
MACMILLAN & CO LTD
NEW YORK · ST MARTIN'S PRESS
1961

MACMILLAN AND COMPANY LIMITED
London Bombay Calcutta Madras Melbourne

THE MACMILLAN COMPANY OF CANADA LIMITED
Toronto

ST MARTIN'S PRESS INC
New York

FOREWORD

It has fallen to me to complete this book without the help and encouragement of my friend and colleague, with whom the work was planned and begun. He made the selection of scenes, and in September 1958, a few weeks before his death, he gave me the rough draft of the Preface and Introduction together with a summary of the omitted passages. Our plan was that I should write the linguistic notes and vocabulary and he would add notes referring to literature, history and mythology and be responsible for the whole. The section on metre was thought of after his death, so I had no opportunity of discussing this with him. Altogether I have felt as if I were blundering on in the dark without his guidance, but others have given me invaluable assistance which I now gratefully acknowledge. Professor E. H. Warmington, of Birkbeck College, very kindly helped me to solve several knotty problems; Mrs. Ariadne Koumari-Sanford, of the University of Thessaloniki, discussed some points in the light of her wide knowledge of Greek, both ancient and modern; and one of my students, Miss M. Anne Ford, gave a good deal of time to the routine work of the vocabulary. The text is Gilbert Murray's Oxford Classical Text (1913), by kind permission of the Clarendon Press. Thanks are due also to Messrs. Sidgwick and Jackson, Ltd., for permission to quote from F. Kinchin Smith's translation of the play. I have consulted the editions of F. A. Paley (1856) and

R. Y. Tyrrell (1897); and I have had considerable help from some manuscript notes in an interleaved Teubner text which bears no name but which I believe to have been the property of Arthur Bernard Cook.

B.J.H.

PREFACE

To the girls and boys who may see this book: It is
written for you, on the assumption that this is your first
Greek play, and in the hope that you will enjoy it.
Greek plays are difficult, but this book gives you the
more difficult portions in English, and the vocabulary
will give you the meaning of all the words in the Greek
passages. There are also notes at the back. Greek plays
are easier than those of Shakespeare because they have
simpler plots, fewer characters and no sub-plots.

The introduction which follows, and which is also
written for you, is intended to tell you what you may
not yet know about Greek plays: for example, how they
started, what they are about, how and when and where
they were acted; and especially about this play, one of
the greatest, which was misunderstood and rarely read
until the late Professor Gilbert Murray, the greatest
Greek scholar in England in the last hundred years,
interpreted it and translated it.

F.K.S.

CONTENTS

INTRODUCTION

1. Why did the Greeks write plays?

Nobody knows how plays began in Greece. Some scholars think they began with prayers to the dead; others, and they are the majority, believe they began with hymns sung at the end of winter to Dionysus, the god not just of wine, as is commonly believed, but of fertility, renewal of life and rebirth in nature at the beginning of spring. The ancient Greeks, like their descendants today, were very poor and depended on the soil for their very existence. They knew, when they sowed the corn seeds or planted the vine shoots, that unless these sprouted and grew there would be no corn, no harvest and no wine, and they would die. Therefore at the end of March every year they held a sacred festival lasting three days in honour of Dionysus, invoking him to make the seeds grow. This festival took the form of religious plays acted in his honour (not unlike the earliest Miracle Plays in England). The plays sprang out of odes called ' dithyrambs ', sung by a group of men in honour of the god; on one occasion one of them stepped out of the group and spoke in reply to the rest. Thus drama was born.

2. What are Greek plays about?

The subjects that the Greek dramatists chose for their plays were almost always connected with the religious stories called ' myths ' which were interwoven with legends of their remote past. It is just as if all modern drama dealt only with stories of the Old Testament and legends of King Arthur and similar heroes. Greek plays deal with stories told in the Iliad and Odyssey of people such as Agamemnon and Odysseus, and with famous characters in other epics which have now been lost; they describe the tragedies that befell men like Oedipus and Heracles and women such as Antigone and Iphigenia. This play describes the fate of the women of Troy immediately after the capture of their city by the Greeks.

3. THE LEGEND BEHIND THIS PLAY

Troy was first named after Trōs, and later after Ilus, its founder, a descendant of Zeus. His son Laomedon employed Apollo and Poseidon, the sea-god, to build the walls, but when they had finished he refused to pay them. Poseidon, therefore, sent a sea-monster against the city. Laomedon sought the help of Heracles, son of Alcmena, who said he would destroy the monster after Laomedon promised to give him his famous horses. Laomedon deceived him too. So Heracles, together with Telamon, king of Salamis, raised an army and sacked the city.

Laomedon had two sons: Tithonus, who was loved by Aurora, goddess of dawn, and became immortal, and Priam, who succeeded him as king of Troy. Neither of these, however, could save the city, nor could Ganymede, brother of Ilus, who was taken up to heaven to be the cup-bearer of Zeus. This is the theme of the choral ode (lines 799–859), describing the first sack of Troy.

Priam married Hecuba (Hecabe) and had a large family, of which Hector, Paris, Polyxena and Cassandra were the most famous. The following tree shows their relationships.

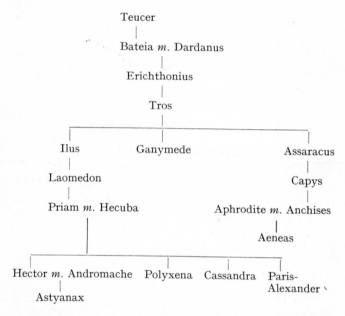

Before Paris was born, Hecuba had a dream that she would bring forth a firebrand whose flames would engulf the whole of Troy. This came true after the riddling fashion of dreams. Paris, when he was a young man and was minding flocks on Mount Ida, was visited by three goddesses—Athena, the goddess of wisdom, Hera, the wife of Zeus, and Aphrodite, the goddess of love. They invited him to decide which of them was the most beautiful. Athena offered him kingship over Greece, Hera sovereignty over Asia, and Aphrodite the most beautiful woman in the world for his wife. Paris gave Aphrodite the prize and with her help made a voyage to Greece and abducted Helen, the wife of Menelaus, king of Sparta.

This was the alleged cause of the Trojan war. In its tenth year Hector was killed by Achilles, the most renowned fighter in the Greek army; he left a widow, Andromache, and a young son, Astyanax. They both come into the play. Troy was taken and sacked, and at this point the play begins. Poseidon had been on Troy's side ever since he had helped to build her walls. He is now on the point of leaving the city to its fate when Athena appears with a request for his help. She has always been the patron goddess of the Greeks, but is now horrified at their inhuman behaviour in the sack of the city. Amongst other atrocities they had murdered Priam on the steps of the altar of Zeus, and Polyxena at the grave of Achilles on the Trojan plain.

4. HOW MUCH TRUTH IS THERE IN THE STORY?

Until the latter part of the nineteenth century scholars all over the world believed that the Trojan war was a fairy tale. A German boy called Heinrich Schliemann, fired by Homer's story in the Iliad, thought otherwise. After beginning life as an apprentice in a grocer's shop and taking jobs in many countries to earn money, he was able to attempt his life's ambition, namely to go and dig for Troy. All the scholars thought him crazy, but he found the actual walls just where Homer said they were, and no scholar today questions this. We therefore now believe that the Trojan war actually took place, and archaeological evidence from objects dug up on the site confirms the traditional date of about 1280 B.C. for the end of the war. Were the characters imaginary? Was there for instance an Agamemnon or a Helen? After discovering Troy, Schliemann went to Mycenae in Greece; after digging he believed he had proved that Agamemnon lived there in a castle whose giant walls can be seen today. Excavation in the last seventy-five years has necessitated the rewriting of the early chapters of Greek history. The discoveries of Sir Arthur Evans in Crete in the first part of this century, which made it almost certain that the story of Theseus and the Minotaur was not merely a legend, and in the last few years the finding of the palace of Nestor at Pylos, leave no doubt that beneath mythology is buried history. Moreover, thanks to the brilliant discoveries of Michael Ventris and others, it is now possible to read the documents discovered at Pylos, which prove to have been written in Greek.

Archaeology has not yet thrown any light on whether there was a Helen, and no one has so far discovered the palace of Menelaus at Sparta, but one day someone may.

5. WHO WAS EURIPIDES AND WHY DID HE WRITE THIS PLAY?

In the earliest Greek plays there was only one actor and a chorus. Athens took the lead in developing drama, both tragedy and comedy, and during the hundred years after the battle of Salamis in 480 B.C. her playwrights produced plays of which the latest is as modern in thought as those of Bernard Shaw. Of these dramatists three are as famous as Shakespeare, and, though individually not perhaps as great, they rank with him. These are Aeschylus, Sophocles and Euripides, who were all Athenians and wrote and produced their plays in Athens. We are told that Aeschylus fought in the battle of Salamis, that Sophocles took part in the boys' chorus commemorating the victory and that Euripides was born on that day. Aeschylus wrote over eighty plays, but only seven have survived. He was a deeply religious man and a profound thinker but made uneasy by the immoral behaviour attributed to the gods in Homer's stories. His greatest play, the Agamemnon, is frequently acted today. It deals with the murder of a man by his wife and the consequences of the crime. The plays of Aeschylus need only two actors, although the characters are more than two; one actor played more than one part, and if three characters had to appear at once only two spoke; the third was an ' extra '. Sophocles introduced a third actor, and his plays (of which only seven survive out of ninety) are therefore more dramatic and easier to act. His Antigone, also frequently acted today, is concerned with the dilemma of a person who has to choose between obeying his or her conscience and obeying the law of the State. We have, fortunately, seventeen plays of Euripides, largely because, though he was not appreciated in his lifetime, he was better understood after his death. His plays also discuss moral problems but with a deeper insight into human behaviour.

In 415 B.C. he wrote The Trojan Women; he chose the theme for the following reasons: Athens was fighting for her life in one of the most disastrous civil wars in history. For years she had been fighting Sparta, a rival state in the south of Greece. Ideals had degenerated, as so often happens in wartime, and Athens had perpetrated a crime which had disturbed him profoundly. The small island of Melos in the Aegean sea had wished to remain neutral since it had no concern in the war. The Athenians refused to accept this; they sent an expedition and, after a long siege, massacred every man there and took all the women and children into slavery. This so horrified Euripides that he wrote The Trojan Women, describing a similar occasion when the Greeks some 700 years before had behaved as brutally after they had captured Troy. The Trojan war was treated by the heroic tradition as one of the most glorious feats of Greek arms, but this play tells the story very differently. It describes the fate of the women after the capture of Troy and reveals their point of view and how it felt to be the conquered side. Euripides took a great risk in writing this play in wartime and criticising his own people. We may well wonder what were the feelings of the audience who had voted for the annihilation of Melos, when there rang through the theatre the words of one of the characters:

' ὦ βάρβαρ' ἐξευρόντες Ἕλληνες κακά. '
(764)

' You Greeks, what barbaric un-Greek tortures you have devised! ' Euripides was a brave man, and only a great people would have been willing to listen to such a stringent invective against themselves during a war in

B

which they were fighting for their lives. Could this happen today?

6. WHERE, WHEN AND HOW WERE GREEK PLAYS ACTED?

A. Greek plays were always acted out of doors. The theatre was scooped out of a hillside, in the shape of a semi-circle. Some theatres were very large, holding at least 20,000 people. One essential difference between an ancient Greek and a modern theatre is that the Greek theatre had in its centre a circular dancing place called the ὀρχήστρα, in which the chorus sang their choral odes and accompanied them with dancing. The earliest Greek theatres had no seats, but by the time this play was produced at Athens in 415 B.C., in the theatre of Dionysus, there were probably wooden seats. These were later replaced by stone ones which are still there today. We do not know much about the stage, but it was very simple, probably consisting of just a platform on which the actors spoke their lines. Behind the stage there was a long wooden hut called σκηνή, where the actors robed themselves. The front of this was painted to represent an appropriate background, a palace, temple or hut. Hence come our words ' scene ' and ' scenery '. The actors were always men, as in Shakespeare's day. They wore large painted masks and high-soled boots and padded clothes in order to be conspicuous to the spectators on the topmost row. With masks, facial expression was impossible; so also was rapid movement with a six-inch clog tied beneath a boot. The actors therefore had to rely entirely on their voices. There was no curtain and the plays were one-act plays performed without an interval. Every important Greek city had its theatre, and the ruins of many can still be seen today. The best preserved is at Epidaurus, where the acoustics are so amazingly good that an actor speaking in a quiet voice can be clearly heard from the highest row of seats, the fiftieth.

B. When were Greek plays acted? You could not go to the theatre every day as you can in London. Greek plays were put on only once a year, at the religious festival in honour of Dionysus at the end of March. The festival lasted for three days, and on each day a chosen dramatist was appointed to produce a cycle of three plays, called a ' trilogy '. The nearest modern equivalent is the Edinburgh Festival, or possibly Oberammergau. Every citizen of Athens would be there, for it was a three-day holiday; those who could not afford the entrance-fee were given free tickets. The first of the three plays would begin at about 7 a.m. and would be followed by two others, almost without a break. Spectators would bring their lunch with them and picnic during the less exciting scenes. In the afternoon there would be a comedy.

C. How did Greek plays differ from the plays of today? We have already mentioned some ways in which they were different, but the greatest difference is this: they were a combination of several things, a religious service (as on Good Friday in Catholic churches), an opera in which music was essential but the words mattered more, a ballet in which no words were spoken but dancing explained the action, and a competition between the three chosen playwrights to decide who was the greatest. Judges were drawn by lot from the audience. Imagine the excitement on the last day when the judges gave their verdict. Did they always make the right choice? Euripides won only the third prize with his Medea. He got no prize for his Trojan Women. We do not know the names of his successful rivals or their plays, because they are lost; we do know, however, that his Trojan Women was the third play of a trilogy of which the first play dealt with a good man condemned by an evil world; the second, called Alexander (another name for Paris), had for its hero a slave. This was unprecedented in a Greek play. We should not form a final opinion about the third act of a trilogy, but though the first two acts are lost beyond recall the final one will, I hope, interest you.

7. HAS THE PLAY ANY MESSAGE FOR US TODAY?

Greek plays, like Shakespeare's tragedies, are concerned with deep moral problems, problems of right and wrong. This play is especially modern because of the attitude to war which it reveals. Euripides was not a pacifist, yet the play contains the following lines:

'Whoever then is wise, should pause before making war,
But if war must come,
A noble death brings honour to a soldier's city;
A coward's death brings nothing but disgrace.'

(400–402)

It is not a pacifist play but the play of a sensitive poet who loved his city (as is obvious from a famous chorus in the Medea) but realised that war brings no solution either to victors or to vanquished. His heart was well-nigh broken by the inhuman acts to which his city had stooped, as we have mentioned in a previous section. He saw that victory alone is not enough, but that it is what victors do with victory that matters. Again and again in the play it is the atrocious acts of the Greek conquerors, his own people, that are hinted at. This message holds true as much today as it did when Euripides wrote the play nearly 2,400 years ago.

8. Metre

English verse-forms depend largely on stress; Greek (and Latin) verse-forms depend largely on quantity, that is, the length of time taken to pronounce the different syllables. For the purpose of metre (measure) only two lengths are recognised, long and short; the usual marks for noting these are – and ᴗ, placed over the syllable. A syllable with a long vowel or diphthong is always long, but a syllable with a short vowel counts as long if the vowel is followed by two or more consonants. (For exceptions see below.) *N.B.* Such a vowel itself remains short; this is obvious in πόντου (o does not change to ω) and less obvious, but still true, in συνθέλω, where the υ of σύν remains short although the syllable is long. When noting combinations of consonants, remember that ζ, ξ and ψ each denote two separate consonantal sounds, but θ, φ and χ do not. Remember also that a vowel with a circumflex accent is long. A syllable containing a short vowel before certain combinations of consonants in the same word may count as long or short. Such a combination of consonants consists of a ' mute ' (β, δ, θ, π, τ, κ, φ, χ) followed by a ' liquid ' (λ, μ, ν, ρ). Thus the first syllable of πατήρ is short but the first of πατρός may be long or short, according to whether it is pronounced πατ-ρός or πα-τρός: either way the α is short.

It is necessary to know these points in order to appreciate the skill of a Greek poet in playing variations, as it were, on a tune. The basic pattern used for most of the dialogue in Tragedy is a line (or verse) of six ' feet ', each of which is an *iamb* (⏑-). Two feet were thought of as making a ' measure ', so the line was called an Iambic Trimeter. In some places in the line a *spondee* (--) occurs instead of the iamb, and sometimes the iamb or spondee is ' resolved ', that is, it has a long syllable replaced by two short ones; the resulting ' resolved ' feet are the *tribrach* (⏑⏑⏑), *anapaest* (⏑⏑-) and *dactyl* (-⏑⏑). The last syllable of the 6th foot is often short. Spondees and resolved feet do not occur in all six positions; the usual scheme, with the different possibilities, is given below, but further variations may be found when proper names occur.

1	2	3	4	5	6
⏑ -	⏑ -	⏑ ‖ -	⏑ ‖ -	⏑ -	⏑⏑̆
- -		-	-		- -
⏑⏑⏑	⏑⏑⏑	⏑ ‖ ⏑⏑	⏑ ‖ ⏑⏑	⏑⏑⏑	
- ⏑⏑		-	⏑⏑		
⏑⏑ -					

The double upright lines denote the ' Caesura ', or cut in the line, between two words; it does not necessarily occur in both the 3rd and the 4th feet.

The lyric metres are too complicated to be explained here. The reader will find them treated fully in Tyrrell's edition of the Troades (Macmillan, 1897). But one other metre which is used in these Selections is simpler and can be explained briefly. It is the Trochaic Tetrameter Catalectic used in lines 444–461. The basic pattern is the *trochee* (-◡) repeated seven times and followed by an extra syllable. The following scheme shows the variations occurring in this passage.

According to Aristotle, this was the original metre of dialogue.

In the notes at the back attention is drawn to resolved feet where they occur, and also to a few words of which the pronunciation varies: e.g. θεός may be either one or two syllables, and πόλεως may be either two or three. Comments on metre are given in brackets.

ΤΡΩΙΑΔΕΣ
THE TROJAN WOMEN

ΤΑ ΤΟΥ ΔΡΑΜΑΤΟΣ ΠΡΟΣΩΠΑ
CHARACTERS OF THE PLAY

ΠΟΣΕΙΔΩΝ,	the God Poseidon
ΑΘΗΝΑ,	the Goddess Athena
ΕΚΑΒΗ,	Hecuba (or Hecabe), Queen of Troy
ΧΟΡΟΣ ΑΙΧΜΑΛΩΤΙΔΩΝ	
ΤΡΩΙΑΔΩΝ,	Chorus of captive Trojan women
ΤΑΛΘΥΒΙΟΣ,	Talthybius, a Greek herald
ΚΑΣΑΝΔΡΑ,	Cassandra, daughter of Hecuba
ΑΝΔΡΟΜΑΧΗ,	Andromache, daughter-in-law of Hecuba
ΑΣΤΥΑΝΑΞ,	Astyanax, her son
ΜΕΝΕΛΑΟΣ,	Menelaus, a Greek general
ΕΛΕΝΗ,	Helen, his wife
	Soldiers and Attendants

THE TROJAN WOMEN

*Lines 1–97. The scene opens on the battlefield just outside the
walls of Troy, which has been sacked by the Greeks after a
ten years' war and a terrible battle. The wooden horse had
let the Greeks right into the city of Troy. The Greek soldiers
had behaved cruelly and disgracefully in killing the men and
boys and rounding up the women and girls to take them to be
slaves in their country. The captives are herded in huts
awaiting their fate.*

*The play begins with Poseidon, the god of the sea, who had
helped to build the city walls and had long been a friend of
Troy, bewailing the destruction of his city.*

*Athena, goddess of the Greeks, has changed her allegiance,
and is now on the side of Troy, disgusted by the brutality
which the Greeks have shown. In the following dialogue she
urges Poseidon to help her punish the Greeks by using his
power to destroy their fleet with his thunderbolts on its way
home.*

ΠΟΣΕΙΔΩΝ

῞Ηκω λιπὼν Αἴγαιον ἁλμυρὸν βάθος
πόντου Ποσειδῶν, ἔνθα Νηρῄδων χοροὶ
κάλλιστον ἴχνος ἐξελίσσουσιν ποδός.
ἐξ οὗ γὰρ ἀμφὶ τήνδε Τρωικὴν χθόνα
Φοῖβός τε κἀγὼ λαΐνους πύργους πέριξ   5
ὀρθοῖσιν ἔθεμεν κανόσιν, οὔποτ᾽ ἐκ φρενῶν
εὔνοι᾽ ἀπέστη τῶν ἐμῶν Φρυγῶν πόλει·
ἥ νῦν καπνοῦται καὶ πρὸς Ἀργείου δορὸς
ὄλωλε πορθηθεῖσ᾽· ὁ γὰρ Παρνάσιος
Φωκεὺς Ἐπειός, μηχαναῖσι Παλλάδος   10

1

ἐγκύμον' ἵππον τευχέων ξυναρμόσας,
πύργων ἔπεμψεν ἐντὸς ὀλέθριον βρέτας·
[ὅθεν πρὸς ἀνδρῶν ὑστέρων κεκλήσεται
Δούρειος Ἵππος, κρυπτὸν ἀμπισχὼν δόρυ.]
    ἔρημα δ' ἄλση καὶ θεῶν ἀνάκτορα   15
φόνῳ καταρρεῖ· πρὸς δὲ κρηπῖδος βάθροις
πέπτωκε Πρίαμος Ζηνὸς ἑρκείου θανών.
πολὺς δὲ χρυσὸς Φρύγιά τε σκυλεύματα
πρὸς ναῦς Ἀχαιῶν πέμπεται· μένουσι δὲ
πρύμνηθεν οὖρον, ὡς δεκασπόρῳ χρόνῳ   20
ἀλόχους τε καὶ τέκν' εἰσίδωσιν ἄσμενοι,
οἳ τήνδ' ἐπεστράτευσαν Ἕλληνες πόλιν.
ἐγὼ δέ—νικῶμαι γὰρ Ἀργείας θεοῦ
Ἥρας Ἀθάνας θ', αἳ συνεξεῖλον Φρύγας—
λείπω τὸ κλεινὸν Ἴλιον βωμούς τ' ἐμούς·   25
ἐρημία γὰρ πόλιν ὅταν λάβῃ κακή,
νοσεῖ τὰ τῶν θεῶν οὐδὲ τιμᾶσθαι θέλει.
πολλοῖς δὲ κωκυτοῖσιν αἰχμαλωτίδων
βοᾷ Σκάμανδρος δεσπότας κληρουμένων.
καὶ τὰς μὲν Ἀρκάς, τὰς δὲ Θεσσαλὸς λεὼς   30
εἴληχ' Ἀθηναίων τε Θησεῖδαι πρόμοι.
ὅσαι δ' ἄκληροι Τρῳάδων, ὑπὸ στέγαις
ταῖσδ' εἰσί, τοῖς πρώτοισιν ἐξῃρημέναι
στρατοῦ, σὺν αὐταῖς δ' ἡ Λάκαινα Τυνδαρὶς
Ἑλένη, νομισθεῖσ' αἰχμάλωτος ἐνδίκως.   35
    τὴν δ' ἀθλίαν τήνδ' εἴ τις εἰσορᾶν θέλει,
πάρεστιν, Ἑκάβην κειμένην πυλῶν πάρος,
δάκρυα χέουσαν πολλὰ καὶ πολλῶν ὕπερ·
ἣ παῖς μὲν ἀμφὶ μνῆμ' Ἀχιλλείου τάφου
λάθρα τέθνηκε τλημόνως Πολυξένη·   40
φροῦδος δὲ Πρίαμος καὶ τέκν'· ἣν δὲ παρθένον
μεθῆκ' Ἀπόλλων δρομάδα Κασάνδραν ἄναξ,

τὸ τοῦ θεοῦ τε παραλιπὼν τό τ' εὐσεβὲς
γαμεῖ βιαίως σκότιον Ἀγαμέμνων λέχος.

   ἀλλ', ὦ ποτ' εὐτυχοῦσα, χαῖρέ μοι, πόλις   45
ξεστόν τε πύργωμ'· εἴ σε μὴ διώλεσεν
Παλλὰς Διὸς παῖς, ἦσθ' ἂν ἐν βάθροις ἔτι.

ΑΘΗΝΑ

   ἔξεστι τὸν γένει μὲν ἄγχιστον πατρὸς
μέγαν τε δαίμον' ἐν θεοῖς τε τίμιον,
λύσασαν ἔχθραν τὴν πάρος, προσεννέπειν;   50
Πο. ἔξεστιν· αἱ γὰρ συγγενεῖς ὁμιλίαι,
ἄνασσ' Ἀθάνα, φίλτρον οὐ σμικρὸν φρενῶν.
Αθ. ἐπήνεσ' ὀργὰς ἠπίους· φέρω δὲ σοὶ
κοινοὺς ἐμαυτῇ τ' ἐς μέσον λόγους, ἄναξ.
Πο. μῶν ἐκ θεῶν του καινὸν ἀγγελεῖς ἔπος,   55
ἢ Ζηνὸς ἢ καὶ δαιμόνων τινὸς πάρα;
Αθ. οὔκ, ἀλλὰ Τροίας οὕνεκ', ἔνθα βαίνομεν,
πρὸς σὴν ἀφῖγμαι δύναμιν, ὡς κοινὴν λάβω.
Πο. ἦ πού νιν, ἔχθραν τὴν πρὶν ἐκβαλοῦσα, νῦν
ἐς οἶκτον ἦλθες πυρὶ κατηθαλωμένης;   60
Αθ. ἐκεῖσε πρῶτ' ἄνελθε· κοινώσῃ λόγους
καὶ συνθελήσεις ἃν ἐγὼ πρᾶξαι θέλω;
Πο. μάλιστ'· ἀτὰρ δὴ καὶ τὸ σὸν θέλω μαθεῖν·
πότερον Ἀχαιῶν ἦλθες οὕνεκ' ἢ Φρυγῶν;
Αθ. τοὺς μὲν πρὶν ἐχθροὺς Τρῶας εὐφρᾶναι θέλω,   65
στρατῷ δ' Ἀχαιῶν νόστον ἐμβαλεῖν πικρόν.
Πο. τί δ' ὧδε πηδᾷς ἄλλοτ' εἰς ἄλλους τρόπους
μισεῖς τε λίαν καὶ φιλεῖς ὃν ἂν τύχῃς;
Αθ. οὐκ οἶσθ' ὑβρισθεῖσάν με καὶ ναοὺς ἐμούς;
Πο. οἶδ', ἡνίκ' Αἴας εἷλκε Κασάνδραν βίᾳ.   70
Αθ. κοὐδέν γ' Ἀχαιῶν ἔπαθεν οὐδ' ἤκουσ' ὕπο.
Πο. καὶ μὴν ἔπερσάν γ' Ἴλιον τῷ σῷ σθένει.

Αθ. τοιγάρ σφε σὺν σοὶ βούλομαι δρᾶσαι κακῶς.

Πο. ἕτοιμ᾽ἃ βούλῃ τἀπ᾽ ἐμοῦ. δράσεις δὲ τί;

Αθ. δύσνοστον αὐτοῖς νόστον ἐμβαλεῖν θέλω. 75

Πο. ἐν γῇ μενόντων ἢ καθ᾽ ἁλμυρὰν ἅλα;

Αθ. ὅταν πρὸς οἴκους ναυστολῶσ᾽ ἀπ᾽ Ἰλίου.
καὶ Ζεὺς μὲν ὄμβρον καὶ χάλαζαν ἄσπετον
πέμψει, δνοφώδη τ᾽ αἰθέρος φυσήματα·
ἐμοὶ δὲ δώσειν φησὶ πῦρ κεραύνιον, 80
βάλλειν Ἀχαιοὺς ναῦς τε πιμπράναι πυρί.
σὺ δ᾽ αὖ, τὸ σόν, παράσχες Αἰγαῖον πόρον
τρικυμίαις βρέμοντα καὶ δίναις ἁλός,
πλῆσον δὲ νεκρῶν κοῖλον Εὐβοίας μυχόν,
ὡς ἂν τὸ λοιπὸν τἄμ᾽ ἀνάκτορ᾽ εὐσεβεῖν 85
εἰδῶσ᾽ Ἀχαιοί, θεούς τε τοὺς ἄλλους σέβειν.

Πο. ἔσται τάδ᾽· ἡ χάρις γὰρ οὐ μακρῶν λόγων
δεῖται· ταράξω πέλαγος Αἰγαίας ἁλός.
ἀκταὶ δὲ Μυκόνου Δήλιοί τε χοιράδες
Σκῦρός τε Λῆμνός θ᾽ αἱ Καφήρειοί τ᾽ ἄκραι 90
πολλῶν θανόντων σώμαθ᾽ ἕξουσιν νεκρῶν.
ἀλλ᾽ ἕρπ᾽ Ὄλυμπον; καὶ κεραυνίους βολὰς
λαβοῦσα πατρὸς ἐκ χερῶν καραδόκει,
ὅταν στράτευμ᾽ Ἀργεῖον ἐξιῇ κάλως.

μῶρος δὲ θνητῶν ὅστις ἐκπορθεῖ πόλεις, 95
ναούς τε τύμβους θ᾽, ἱερὰ τῶν κεκμηκότων,
ἐρημίᾳ δοὺς αὐτὸς ὤλεθ᾽ ὕστερον.

Lines 98–229. As Poseidon and Athena disappear in the early dawn, Hecuba, the Queen of Troy, whose husband, Priam, has just been murdered, is seen slowly raising her head from the ground where she has lain all night. She speaks thus: ' Of all women I am most unhappy. I am Queen of Troy, yet there is no Troy. My country, children, husband, all are gone. I came to the palace a queen, I am dragged away a slave.'

*She rises, and looking towards the Greek ships laments
their coming to Troy to take back Menelaus' wife Helen, who
was the cause of the war. She calls her a murderess for having
caused the death of her husband Priam and her children. She
turns to the captive women in the huts and continues:
' Unhappy wives of Trojan soldiers, weep, for Troy is a
smoking ruin, and I am anguished for my country.'*

*In their distress the women ask Hecuba if she knows where
they will be sent, but she herself is unaware. Talthybius, the
Greek herald, enters bringing the dreaded news.*

Lines 230–393. *Hecuba and the Chorus anxiously question
Talthybius and learn that Cassandra is to be Agamemnon's
mistress. He tells them that Polyxena is already dead, but
they cannot understand; Andromache is to go to Achilles'
son, and Hecuba herself to Odysseus. The mad Cassandra
enters with a lighted torch (l. 306) and prophesies in a
frenzy. Presently (l. 365) she grows calmer; she turns from the
future to the past, and compares sufferings of Trojans and
Greeks.*

ΧΟΡΟΣ

καὶ μὴν Δαναῶν ὅδ' ἀπὸ στρατιᾶς   230
κῆρυξ, νεοχμῶν μύθων ταμίας,
στείχει ταχύπουν ἴχνος ἐξανύων.
τί φέρει; τί λέγει; δοῦλαι γὰρ δὴ
    Δωρίδος ἐσμὲν χθονὸς ἤδη.

ΤΑΛΘΥΒΙΟΣ

Ἑκάβη, πυκνὰς γὰρ οἶσθά μ' ἐς Τροίαν ὁδοὺς   235
ἐλθόντα κήρυκ' ἐξ Ἀχαικοῦ στρατοῦ,
ἐγνωσμένος δὲ καὶ πάροιθέ σοι, γύναι,
Ταλθύβιος ἥκω καινὸν ἀγγελῶν λόγον.
Εκ. ⟨αἰαῖ,⟩ τόδε
    τόδε, φίλαι Τρῳάδες, ὃ φόβος ἦν πάλαι.
Τα. ἤδη κεκλήρωσθ', εἰ τόδ' ἦν ὑμῖν φόβος.   240

Εκ.   αἰαῖ, τίν' ἢ
     Θεσσαλίας πόλιν ἢ
     Φθιάδος εἶπας ἢ Καδμείας χθονός;
Τα. κατ' ἄνδρ' ἑκάστη κοὐχ ὁμοῦ λελόγχατε.
Εκ.   τίν' ἄρα τίς ἔλαχε; τίνα πότμος εὐτυχὴς
     Ἰλιάδων μένει;   245
Τα. οἶδ'· ἀλλ' ἕκαστα πυνθάνου, μὴ πάνθ' ὁμοῦ.
Εκ.   τοὐμὸν τίς ἆρ'
     ἔλαχε τέκος, ἔνεπε, τλάμονα Κασάνδραν;
Τα. ἐξαίρετόν νιν ἔλαβεν Ἀγαμέμνων ἄναξ.
Εκ.   ἦ τᾷ Λακεδαιμονίᾳ νύμφᾳ
     δούλαν; ἰώ μοί μοι.   250
Τα. οὔκ, ἀλλὰ λέκτρων σκότια νυμφευτήρια.
Εκ.   ἦ τὰν τοῦ Φοίβου παρθένον, ᾇ γέρας ὁ
     χρυσοκόμας ἔδωκ' ἄλεκτρον ζόαν;
Τα. ἔρως ἐτόξευσ' αὐτὸν ἐνθέου κόρης.   255
Εκ.   ῥῖπτε, τέκνον, ζαθέους κλῇ-
     δας καί ἀπὸ χροὸς ἐνδυ-
     τῶν στεφέων ἱεροὺς στολμούς.
Τα. οὐ γὰρ μέγ' αὐτῇ βασιλικῶν λέκτρων τυχεῖν;   259
Εκ.   τί δ' ὁ νεοχμὸν ἀπ' ἐμέθεν ἐλάβετε τέκος, ποῦ μοι;
Τα. Πολυξένην ἔλεξας, ἢ τίν' ἱστορεῖς;
Εκ.   ταύταν· τῷ πάλος ἔζευξεν;
Τα. τύμβῳ τέτακται προσπολεῖν Ἀχιλλέως.
Εκ.   ὤμοι ἐγώ· τάφῳ πρόσπολον ἐτεκόμαν.   265
     ἀτὰρ τίς ὅδ' ἢ νόμος ἢ τί
     θέσμιον, ὦ φίλος, Ἑλλάνων;
Τα. εὐδαιμόνιζε παῖδα σήν· ἔχει καλῶς.
Εκ.   τί τόδ' ἔλακες; ἆρά μοι ἀέλιον λεύσσει;
Τα. ἔχει πότμος νιν, ὥστ' ἀπηλλάχθαι πόνων.   270
Εκ.   τί δ' ἁ τοῦ χαλκεομήστορος Ἕκτορος δάμαρ,
     Ἀνδρομάχα τάλαινα, τίν' ἔχει τύχαν;

Τα.   καί τήνδ' 'Αχιλλέως ἔλαβε παῖς ἐξαίρετον.

Εκ.   ἐγὼ δὲ τῷ
      πρόσπολος ἁ τριτοβάμονος χερὶ   275
      δευομένα βάκτρου γεραιῷ κάρᾳ;

Τα.   'Ιθάκης 'Οδυσσεὺς ἔλαχ' ἄναξ δούλην σ' ἔχειν.

Εκ.   ἒ ἔ.
      ἄρασσε κρᾶτα κούριμον,
      ἕλκ' ὀνύχεσσι δίπτυχον παρειάν.   280
      ἰώ μοί μοι.
         μυσαρῷ δολίῳ λέλογχα φωτὶ δουλεύειν,
      πολεμίῳ δίκας, παρανόμῳ δάκει,
      ὃς πάντα τἀκεῖθεν ἐνθάδ ⟨ε στρέφει, τὰ δ'⟩   285
         ἀντίπαλ' αὖθις ἐκεῖσε διπτύχῳ γλώσσᾳ
      φίλα τὰ πρότερ' ἄφιλα τιθέμενος πάντων.
      γοᾶσθ', ὦ Τρῳάδες, με.
      βέβακα δύσποτμος. [οἴχομαι] ἁ
      τάλαινα, δυστυχεστάτῳ   290
      προσέπεσον κλήρῳ.

Χο.   τὸ μὲν σὸν οἶσθα, πότνια, τὰς δ' ἐμὰς τύχας
      τίς ἆρ' 'Αχαιῶν ἢ τίς 'Ελλήνων ἔχει;

Τα.   ἴτ', ἐκκομίζειν δεῦρο Κασάνδραν χρεὼν
      ὅσον τάχιστα, δμῶες, ὡς στρατηλάτῃ   295
      ἐς χεῖρα δούς νιν, εἶτα τὰς εἰληγμένας
      καὶ τοῖσιν ἄλλοις αἰχμαλωτίδων ἄγω.
         ἔα· τί πεύκης ἔνδον αἴθεται σέλας;
      πιμπρᾶσιν—ἢ τί δρῶσι—Τρῳάδες μυχούς,
      ὡς ἐξάγεσθαι τῆσδε μέλλουσαι χθονὸς   300
      πρὸς "Αργος, αὑτῶν τ' ἐκπυροῦσι σώματα
      θανεῖν θέλουσαι; κάρτα τοι τοὐλεύθερον
      ἐν τοῖς τοιούτοις δυσλόφως φέρει κακά.
         ἄνοιγ' ἄνοιγε, μὴ τὸ ταῖσδε πρόσφορον

ἐχθρὸν δ' Ἀχαιοῖς εἰς ἔμ' αἰτίαν βάλῃ. 305

Εκ. οὐκ ἔστιν, οὐ πιμπρᾶσιν, ἀλλὰ παῖς ἐμὴ
μαινὰς θοάζει δεῦρο Κασάνδρα δρόμῳ.

ΚΑΣΑΝΔΡΑ

Ἄνεχε· πάρεχε.
φῶς φέρ', ὦ· σέβω· φλέγω—ἰδού, ἰδού—
λαμπάσι τόδ' ἱερόν.
ὦ Ὑμέναι' ἄναξ· 310
μακάριος ὁ γαμέτας·
μακαρία δ' ἐγὼ βασιλικοῖς λέκτροις
κατ' Ἄργος ἁ γαμουμένα.
Ὑμήν, ὦ Ὑμέναι' ἄναξ.
ἐπεὶ σύ, μᾶτερ, ἐπὶ δάκρυσι καὶ 315
γόοισι τὸν θανόντα πατέρα πατρίδα τε
φίλαν καταστένους' ἔχεις,
ἐγὼ δ' ἐπὶ γάμοις ἐμοῖς
ἀναφλέγω πυρὸς φῶς 320
ἐς αὐγάν, ἐς αἴγλαν,
διδοῦσ', ὦ Ὑμέναιε, σοί,
διδοῦσ', ὦ Ἑκάτα, φάος,
παρθένων ἐπὶ λέκτροις
ᾇ νόμος ἔχει.

πάλλε πόδα. 325
αἰθέριον ἄναγε χορόν· εὐάν, εὐοῖ·
ὡς ἐπὶ πατρὸς ἐμοῦ
μακαριωτάταις
τύχαις· ὁ χορὸς ὅσιος.
ἄγε σύ, Φοῖβε, νῦν· κατὰ σὸν ἐν δάφναις
ἀνάκτορον θυηπολῶ, 330
Ὑμήν, ὦ Ὑμέναι', Ὑμήν.
χόρευε, μᾶτερ, ἀναγέλασον·

ἔλισσε τᾷδ' ἐκεῖσε μετ' ἐμέθεν ποδῶν
φέρουσα φιλτάταν βάσιν.
βοάσαθ' Ὑμέναιον, ὤ,   335
μακαρίαις ἀοιδαῖς
ἰαχαῖς τε νύμφαν.
ἴτ', ὦ καλλίπεπλοι Φρυγῶν
κόραι, μέλπετ' ἐμῶν γάμων
τὸν πεπρωμένον εὐνᾷ   340
πόσιν ἐμέθεν.

Χο. βασίλεια, βακχεύουσαν οὐ λήψῃ κόρην,
μὴ κοῦφον αἴρῃ βῆμ' ἐς Ἀργείων στρατόν;
Εκ. Ἥφαιστε, δᾳδουχεῖς μὲν ἐν γάμοις βροτῶν,
ἀτὰρ λυγράν γε τήνδ' ἀναιθύσσεις φλόγα
ἔξω τε μεγάλων ἐλπίδων.
                οἴμοι, τέκνον,   345
ὡς οὐχ ὑπ' αἰχμῆς ⟨σ'⟩ οὐδ' ὑπ' Ἀργείου δορὸς
γάμους γαμεῖσθαι τούσδ' ἐδόξαζόν ποτε.
παράδος ἐμοί φῶς· οὐ γὰρ ὀρθὰ πυρφορεῖς
μαινὰς θοάζουσ', οὐδέ σ' αἱ τύχαι, τέκνον,
†ἐσωφρονήκασ'†, ἀλλ' ἔτ' ἐν ταὐτῷ μένεις.   350
ἐσφέρετε πεύκας, δάκρυά τ' ἀνταλλάξατε
τοῖς τῆσδε μέλεσι, Τρῳάδες, γαμηλίοις.
Κα. μῆτερ, πύκαζε κρᾶτ' ἐμὸν νικηφόρον,
καὶ χαῖρε τοῖς ἐμοῖσι βασιλικοῖς γάμοις·
καὶ πέμπε, κἂν μὴ τἀμά σοι πρόθυμά γ' ᾖ,   355
ὤθει βιαίως· εἰ γὰρ ἔστι Λοξίας,
Ἑλένης γαμεῖ με δυσχερέστερον γάμον
ὁ τῶν Ἀχαιῶν κλεινὸς Ἀγαμέμνων ἄναξ.
κτενῶ γὰρ αὐτόν, κἀντιπορθήσω δόμους
ποινὰς ἀδελφῶν καὶ πατρὸς λαβοῦσ' ἐμοῦ ...   360
ἀλλ' ἅττ' ἐάσω· πέλεκυν οὐχ ὑμνήσομεν,

c

ὃς ἐς τράχηλον τὸν ἐμὸν εἶσι χἀτέρων·
μητροκτόνους τ᾽ ἀγῶνας, οὓς οὑμοὶ γάμοι
θήσουσιν, οἴκων τ᾽ Ἀτρέως ἀνάστασιν.

πόλιν δὲ δείξω τήνδε μακαριωτέραν   365
ἢ τοὺς Ἀχαιούς, ἔνθεος μέν, ἀλλ᾽ ὅμως
τοσόνδε γ᾽ ἔξω στήσομαι βακχευμάτων·
οἳ διὰ μίαν γυναῖκα καὶ μίαν Κύπριν,
θηρῶντες Ἑλένην, μυρίους ἀπώλεσαν.
ὁ δὲ στρατηγὸς ὁ σοφὸς ἐχθίστων ὕπερ   370
τὰ φίλτατ᾽ ὤλεσ᾽, ἡδονὰς τὰς οἴκοθεν
τέκνων ἀδελφῷ δοὺς γυναικὸς οὕνεκα,
καὶ ταῦθ᾽ ἑκούσης κοὐ βίᾳ λελησμένης.
ἐπεὶ δ᾽ ἐπ᾽ ἀκτὰς ἤλυθον Σκαμανδρίους,
ἔθνησκον, οὐ γῆς ὅρι᾽ ἀποστερούμενοι   375
οὐδ᾽ ὑψίπυργον πατρίδ᾽· οὓς δ᾽ Ἄρης ἕλοι,
οὐ παῖδας εἶδον, οὐ δάμαρτος ἐν χεροῖν
πέπλοις συνεστάλησαν, ἐν ξένῃ δὲ γῇ
κεῖνται. τὰ δ᾽ οἴκοι τοῖσδ᾽ ὅμοι᾽ ἐγίγνετο·
χῆραί τ᾽ ἔθνησκον, οἳ δ᾽ ἄπαιδες ἐν δόμοις   380
ἄλλοις τέκν᾽ ἐκθρέψαντες· οὐδὲ πρὸς τάφοις
ἔσθ᾽ ὅστις αὐτῶν αἷμα γῇ δωρήσεται.
ἦ τοῦδ᾽ ἐπαίνου τὸ στράτευμ᾽ ἐπάξιον.—

σιγᾶν ἄμεινον τἀσχρά, μηδὲ μοῦσά μοι
γένοιτ᾽ ἀοιδὸς ἥτις ὑμνήσει κακά.   385

Τρῶες δὲ πρῶτον μέν, τὸ κάλλιστον κλέος,
ὑπὲρ πάτρας ἔθνησκον· οὓς δ᾽ ἕλοι δόρυ,
νεκροί γ᾽ ἐς οἴκους φερόμενοι φίλων ὕπο
ἐν γῇ πατρῴᾳ περιβολὰς εἶχον χθονός,
χερσὶν περισταλέντες ὧν ἐχρῆν ὕπο·   390
ὅσοι δὲ μὴ θάνοιεν ἐν μάχῃ Φρυγῶν,
ἀεὶ κατ᾽ ἦμαρ σὺν δάμαρτι καὶ τέκνοις
ᾤκουν, Ἀχαιοῖς ὧν ἀπῆσαν ἡδοναί.

*Lines 394–443.   Cassandra continues her argument, proclaiming
the good fortune of the Trojans despite their suffering.   Her
thoughts turn to her dead brother Hector, ' the bravest of the
brave,' who, she says, would never have become famous had it
not been for the war.   Then, in striking language, she reveals
the futility of war.   She tells her mother not to grieve and
foretells the destruction of their captors through her marriage
to Agamemnon.   This annoys Talthybius, who says she is
mad and orders her to be taken to the ships and Hecuba to
follow when Odysseus commands.*

*Cassandra prophesies the ten years' ' tormented travel '
that Odysseus will undergo before he reaches his home in
Ithaca.*

*Lines 444–461.   Cassandra prophesies Agamemnon's fate and
her own.*

ΚΑΣΑΝΔΡΑ

ἀλλὰ γὰρ τί τοὺς 'Οδυσσέως ἐξακοντίζω πόνους;
στεῖχ' ὅπως τάχιστ'· ἐς "Αιδου νυμφίῳ γημώμεθα. 445
ἦ κακὸς κακῶς ταφήσῃ νυκτός, οὐκ ἐν ἡμέρᾳ,
ὦ δοκῶν σεμνόν τι πράσσειν, Δαναϊδῶν ἀρχηγέτα.
κἀμέ τοι νεκρὸν φάραγγες γυμνάδ' ἐκβεβλημένην
ὕδατι χειμάρρῳ ῥέουσαι, νυμφίου πέλας τάφου,
θηρσὶ δώσουσιν δάσασθαι, τὴν 'Απόλλωνος λάτριν. 450
ὦ στέφη τοῦ φιλτάτου μοι θεῶν, ἀγάλματ' εὔια,
χαίρετ'· ἐκλέλοιφ' ἑορτάς, αἷς πάροιθ' ἠγαλλόμην.
ἴτ' ἀπ' ἐμοῦ χρωτὸς σπαραγμοῖς, ὡς ἔτ' οὖσ' ἁγνὴ χρόα
δῶ θοαῖς αὔραις φέρεσθαί σοι τάδ', ὦ μαντεῖ' ἄναξ.
    ποῦ σκάφος τὸ τοῦ στρατηγοῦ; ποῖ ποτ' ἐμβαίνειν
        με χρή;   455
οὐκέτ' ἂν φθάνοις ἂν αὔραν ἱστίοις καραδοκῶν,
ὡς μίαν τριῶν 'Ερινὺν τῆσδέ μ' ἐξάξων χθονός.
χαῖρέ μοι, μῆτερ· δακρύσῃς μηδέν· ὦ φίλη πατρίς
οἵ τε γῆς ἔνερθ' ἀδελφοί χὠ τεκὼν ἡμᾶς πατήρ,

οὐ μακρὰν δέξεσθέ μ'· ἥξω δ' ἐς νεκροὺς νικηφόρος 460
καὶ δόμους πέρσασ' 'Ατρειδῶν, ὧν ἀπωλόμεσθ' ὕπο.

*Lines 462–504. Cassandra goes out and Hecuba falls to the
ground. She recalls her previous joys and contrasts them
with her present misfortunes. She has seen her sons killed in
battle by the Greeks, her husband murdered and her daughters
now dragged away. ' And I shall be taken to Greece ', she
says, ' I, Queen of Troy, to become a door-keeper and a
slave.'*

*Lines 505–577. Hecuba asks the Chorus to leave her alone to die.
They sing of the wooden horse and of the last night of Troy.
They see Andromache approaching, and wake Hecuba from
her silence. (The song of the Chorus, ll. 511–567, is translated in the Appendix.)*

ΕΚΑΒΗ

    τί δῆτά μ' ὀρθοῦτ'; ἐλπίδων ποίων ὕπο; 505
    ἄγετε τὸν ἁβρὸν δήποτ' ἐν Τροίᾳ πόδα,
    νῦν δ' ὄντα δοῦλον, στιβάδα πρὸς χαμαιπετῆ
    πέτρινά τε κρήδεμν', ὡς πεσοῦσ' ἀποφθαρῶ
    δακρύοις καταξανθεῖσα. τῶν δ' εὐδαιμόνων
    μηδένα νομίζετ' εὐτυχεῖν, πρὶν ἂν θάνῃ. 510

Χο. ἀμφί μοι "Ιλιον, ὦ [στρ.
    Μοῦσα, καινῶν ὕμνων
  ἄεισον ἐν δακρύοις ᾠδὰν ἐπικήδειον·
    νῦν γὰρ μέλος ἐς Τροίαν ἰαχήσω, 515
    τετραβάμονος ὡς ὑπ' ἀπήνας
  'Αργείων ὀλόμαν τάλαινα δοριάλωτος,
    ὅτ' ἔλιπον ἵππον οὐράνια
    βρέμοντα χρυσεοφάλαρον ἔνο- 520
    πλον ἐν πύλαις 'Αχαιοί·
    ἀνὰ δ' ἐβόασεν λεὼς

Τρωάδος ἀπὸ πέτρας σταθείς·
"Ἴτ', ὦ πεπαυμένοι πόνων,
τόδ' ἱερὸν ἀνάγετε ξόανον   525
'Ιλιάδι Διογενεῖ κόρᾳ.
τίς οὐκ ἔβα νεανίδων,
τίς οὐ γεραιὸς ἐκ δόμων;
κεχαρμένοι δ' ἀοιδαῖς
    δόλιον ἔσχον ἄταν.   530
πᾶσα δὲ γέννα Φρυγῶν   [ἀντ.
πρὸς πύλας ὡρμάθη,
πεύκᾳ ἐν οὐρείᾳ ξεστὸν λόχον 'Αργείων
καί Δαρδανίας ἄταν θεᾷ δώσων,   535
χάριν ἄζυγος ἀμβροτοπώλου·
κλωστοῦ δ' ἀμφιβόλοις λίνοιο ναὸς ὥσει
    σκάφος κελαινόν, εἰς ἕδρανα
λάινα δάπεδά τε φόνια πατρί-   540
    δι Παλλάδος θέσαν θεᾶς.
ἐπὶ δὲ πόνῳ καὶ χαρᾷ
νύχιον ἐπεὶ κνέφας παρῆν,
Λίβυς τε λωτὸς ἐκτύπει
Φρύγιά τε μέλεα, παρθένοι δ'   545
ἀέριον ἀνὰ κρότον ποδῶν
βοὰν ἔμελπον εὔφρον', ἐν
δόμοις δὲ παμφαὲς σέλας
πυρὸς μέλαιναν αἴγλαν
    ⟨ἄκος⟩ ἔδωκεν ὕπνῳ.   550

— ἐγὼ δὲ τὰν ὀρεστέραν
τότ' ἀμφὶ μέλαθρα παρθένον
Διὸς κόραν ἐμελπόμαν
χοροῖσι· φοινία δ' ἀνὰ   555
πτόλιν βοὰ κατεῖχε Περ-

γάμων ἕδρας· βρέφη δὲ φίλι-
α περὶ πέπλους ἔβαλλε μα-
τρὶ χεῖρας ἐπτοημένας·
λόχου δ' ἐξέβαιν' Ἄρης,   560
κόρας ἔργα Παλλάδος.
σφαγαὶ δ' ἀμφιβώμιοι
Φρυγῶν, ἔν τε δεμνίοις
καράτομος ἐρημία
νεανίδων στέφανον ἔφερεν   565
Ἑλλάδι κουροτρόφον,
     Φρυγῶν πατρίδι πένθη.

—   Ἑκάβη, λεύσσεις τήνδ' Ἀνδρομάχην
ξενικοῖς ἐπ' ὄχοις πορθμευομένην;
παρὰ δ' εἰρεσίᾳ μαστῶν ἕπεται   570
φίλος Ἀστυάναξ, Ἕκτορος ἶνις.
ποῖ ποτ' ἀπήνης νώτοισι φέρῃ,
δύστανε γύναι, πάρεδρος χαλκέοις
Ἕκτορος ὅπλοις σκύλοις τε Φρυγῶν
δοριθηράτοις,
οἷσιν Ἀχιλλέως παῖς Φθιώτας   575
στέψει ναοὺς ἀπὸ Τροίας;

Lines 578–633. *Andromache, wife of the dead Hector, enters in a
chariot, carrying in her arms her young son, Astyanax. In
the chariot there is also Hector's armour. Hecuba asks her
where she is going and why. The two take part in a ritualistic
dirge lamenting the agony they have undergone in the sack of
the city. Andromache breaks the news that her sister-in-law,
Polyxena, is also dead, slaughtered at Achilles' tomb.*

Lines 634–656. *Andromache tries to comfort Hecuba, saying that
Polyxena's troubles are over. She turns to the theme of her
own loss, loss of husband, home and honour.*

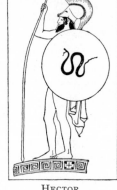

ANDROMACHE WITH
ASTYANAX

HECTOR

from a vase-painting.

ΑΝΔΡΟΜΑΧΗ

ὦ μῆτερ, †ὦ τεκοῦσα†, κάλλιστον λόγον
ἄκουσον, ὥς σοι τέρψιν ἐμβαλῶ φρενί.   635
τὸ μὴ γενέσθαι τῷ θανεῖν ἴσον λέγω,
τοῦ ζῆν δὲ λυπρῶς κρεῖσσόν ἐστι κατθανεῖν.
ἀλγεῖ γὰρ οὐδὲν †τῶν κακῶν ᾐσθημένος·†
ὁ δ᾽ εὐτυχήσας ἐς τὸ δυστυχὲς πεσὼν
ψυχὴν ἀλᾶται τῆς πάροιθ᾽ εὐπραξίας.   640
κείνη δ᾽, ὁμοίως ὥσπερ οὐκ ἰδοῦσα φῶς,
τέθνηκε κοὐδὲν οἶδε τῶν αὑτῆς κακῶν.
ἐγὼ δὲ τοξεύσασα τῆς εὐδοξίας
λαχοῦσα πλεῖον τῆς τύχης ἡμάρτανον.
ἃ γὰρ γυναιξὶ σώφρον᾽ ἔσθ᾽ ηὑρημένα,   645
ταῦτ᾽ ἐξεμόχθουν Ἕκτορος κατὰ στέγας.
πρῶτον μέν, ἔνθα—κἂν προσῇ κἂν μὴ προσῇ
ψόγος γυναιξίν—αὐτὸ τοῦτ᾽ ἐφέλκεται
κακῶς ἀκούειν, ἥτις οὐκ ἔνδον μένει,

τούτου παρεῖσα πόθον ἔμιμνον ἐν δόμοις·   650
ἔσω τε μελάθρων κομψὰ θηλειῶν ἔπη
οὐκ εἰσεφρούμην, τὸν δὲ νοῦν διδάσκαλον
οἴκοθεν ἔχουσα χρηστὸν ἐξήρκουν ἐμοί.
γλώσσης τε σιγὴν ὄμμα θ' ἥσυχον πόσει
παρεῖχον· ἤδη δ' ἀμὲ χρῆν νικᾶν πόσιν,   655
κείνῳ τε νίκην ὧν ἐχρῆν παριέναι.

*Lines 657–706. Andromache continues her description of her
former happiness in Troy with her husband. It is because of
her love for him and her good character, she says, that she has
been chosen as a slave by the son of Achilles, who had killed
her husband. How should she behave towards him? She
despises a woman who, the moment she has lost her husband,
turns to another. Death, she says, would be a happier state,
and Polyxena, whose woe is less than hers, is better off.*

*Hecuba, who has been gazing at the sea, compares her state
to that of sailors on a sinking ship in a storm too violent to
contend with. She advises Andromache to forget Hector and
seek only to please her new master. In this way she may
perhaps save her child Astyanax to redeem and rebuild their
city.*

*Lines 707–789. Talthybius returns with the soldiers. He can
scarcely bring himself to tell Andromache the decision of the
Greeks concerning Astyanax: he is to die. She mourns over
the child and curses Helen. Talthybius reluctantly takes
Astyanax from her.*

ΕΚΑΒΗ

τίν' αὖ δέδορκα τόνδ' 'Αχαϊκὸν λάτριν
στείχοντα καινῶν ἄγγελον βουλευμάτων;

ΤΑΛΘΥΒΙΟΣ

Φρυγῶν ἀρίστου πρίν ποθ' Ἕκτορος δάμαρ,
μή με στυγήσῃς· οὐχ ἑκὼν γὰρ ἀγγελῶ.   710
Δαναῶν δὲ κοινὰ Πελοπιδῶν τ' ἀγγέλματα. . . .

Αν. τί δ' ἔστιν; ὥς μοι φροιμίων ἄρχῃ κακῶν.
Τα. ἔδοξε τόνδε παῖδα ... πῶς εἴπω λόγον;
Αν. μῶν οὐ τὸν αὐτὸν δεσπότην ἡμῖν ἔχειν;
Τα. οὐδεὶς Ἀχαιῶν τοῦδε δεσπόσει ποτέ. 715
Αν. ἀλλ' ἐνθάδ' αὐτοῦ λείψανον Φρυγῶν λιπεῖν;
Τα. οὐκ οἶδ' ὅπως σοι ῥᾳδίως εἴπω κακά.
Αν. ἐπήνεσ' αἰδῶ, πλὴν ἐὰν λέγῃς καλά.
Τα. κτενοῦσι σὸν παῖδ', ὡς πύθῃ κακὸν μέγα.
Αν. οἴμοι, γάμων τόδ' ὡς κλύω μεῖζον κακόν. 720
Τα. νικᾷ δ' Ὀδυσσεὺς ἐν Πανέλλησιν λέγων ...
Αν. αἰαῖ μάλ'· οὐ γὰρ μέτρια πάσχομεν κακά.
Τα. λέξας ἀρίστου παῖδα μὴ τρέφειν πατρὸς ...
Αν. τοιαῦτα νικήσειε τῶν αὐτοῦ πέρι.
Τα. ῥῖψαι δὲ πύργων δεῖν σφε Τρωικῶν ἄπο. 725
    ἀλλ' ὣς γενέσθω, καὶ σοφωτέρα φανῇ·
    μήτ' ἀντέχου τοῦδ', εὐγενῶς δ' ἄλγει κακοῖς,
    μήτε σθένουσα μηδὲν ἰσχύειν δόκει.
    ἔχεις γὰρ ἀλκὴν οὐδαμῇ. σκοπεῖν δὲ χρή·
    πόλις τ' ὄλωλε καὶ πόσις, κρατῇ δὲ σύ, 730
    ἡμεῖς δὲ πρὸς γυναῖκα μάρνασθαι μίαν
    οἷοί τε. τούτων οὕνεκ' οὐ μάχης ἐρᾶν
    οὐδ' αἰσχρὸν οὐδὲν οὐδ' ἐπίφθονόν σε δρᾶν,
    οὐδ' αὖ σ' Ἀχαιοῖς βούλομαι ῥίπτειν ἀράς.
    εἰ γάρ τι λέξεις ὧν χολώσεται στρατός, 735
    οὔτ' ἂν ταφείη παῖς ὅδ' οὔτ' οἴκτου τύχοι.
    σιγῶσα δ' εὖ τε τὰς τύχας κεκτημένη
    τὸν τοῦδε νεκρὸν οὐκ ἄθαπτον ἂν λίποις
    αὐτή τ' Ἀχαιῶν πρευμενεστέρων τύχοις.
Αν. ὦ φίλτατ', ὦ περισσὰ τιμηθεὶς τέκνον, 740
    θανῇ πρὸς ἐχθρῶν μητέρ' ἀθλίαν λιπών,
    ἡ τοῦ πατρὸς δέ σ' εὐγένει' ἀποκτενεῖ,
    ἣ τοῖσιν ἄλλοις γίγνεται σωτηρία,

τὸ δ' ἐσθλὸν οὐκ ἐς καιρὸν ἦλθε σοὶ πατρός.

ὦ λέκτρα τἀμὰ δυστυχῆ τε καὶ γάμοι,   745
οἷς ἦλθον ἐς μέλαθρον Ἕκτορός ποτε,
οὐ σφάγιον υἱὸν Δαναΐδαις τέξουσ' ἐμόν,
ἀλλ' ὡς τύραννον Ἀσιάδος πολυσπόρου.
ὦ παῖ, δακρύεις· αἰσθάνῃ κακῶν σέθεν;
τί μου δέδραξαι χερσὶ κἀντέχῃ πέπλων,   750
νεοσσὸς ὡσεὶ πτέρυγας ἐσπίτνων ἐμάς;
οὐκ εἶσιν Ἕκτωρ κλεινὸν ἁρπάσας δόρυ
γῆς ἐξανελθὼν σοὶ φέρων σωτηρίαν,
οὐ συγγένεια πατρός, οὐκ ἰσχὺς Φρυγῶν·
λυγρὸν δὲ πήδημ' ἐς τράχηλον ὑψόθεν   755
πεσὼν ἀνοίκτως, πνεῦμ' ἀπορρήξεις σέθεν.
ὦ νέον ὑπαγκάλισμα μητρὶ φίλτατον,
ὦ χρωτὸς ἡδὺ πνεῦμα· διὰ κενῆς ἄρα
ἐν σπαργάνοις σε μαστὸς ἐξέθρεψ' ὅδε,
μάτην δ' ἐμόχθουν καὶ κατεξάνθην πόνοις.   760
νῦν—οὔποτ' αὖθις—μητέρ' ἀσπάζου σέθεν,
πρόσπιτνε τὴν τεκοῦσαν, ἀμφὶ δ' ὠλένας
ἕλισσ' ἐμοῖς νώτοισι καὶ στόμ' ἅρμοσον.

ὦ βάρβαρ' ἐξευρόντες Ἕλληνες κακά,
τί τόνδε παῖδα κτείνετ' οὐδὲν αἴτιον;   765
ὦ Τυνδάρειον ἔρνος, οὔποτ' εἶ Διός,
πολλῶν δὲ πατέρων φημί σ' ἐκπεφυκέναι,
Ἀλάστορος μὲν πρῶτον, εἶτα δὲ Φθόνου,
Φόνου τε Θανάτου θ' ὅσα τε γῆ τρέφει κακά.
οὐ γάρ ποτ' αὐχῶ Ζῆνά γ' ἐκφῦσαί σ' ἐγώ,   770
πολλοῖσι κῆρα βαρβάροις Ἕλλησί τε.
ὄλοιο· καλλίστων γὰρ ὀμμάτων ἄπο
αἰσχρῶς τὰ κλεινὰ πεδί' ἀπώλεσας Φρυγῶν.
⟨ἀλλ'⟩ ἄγετε φέρετε ῥίπτετ', εἰ ῥίπτειν δοκεῖ·
δαίνυσθε τοῦδε σάρκας. ἔκ τε γὰρ θεῶν   775

διολλύμεσθα, παιδί τ' οὐ δυναίμεθ' ἂν
θάνατον ἀρῆξαι. κρύπτετ' ἄθλιον δέμας
καὶ ῥίπτετ' ἐς ναῦς· ἐπὶ καλὸν γὰρ ἔρχομαι
ὑμέναιον, ἀπολέσασα τοὐμαυτῆς τέκνον.

Χο. τάλαινα Τροία, μυρίους ἀπώλεσας   780
μιᾶς γυναικὸς καὶ λέχους στυγνοῦ χάριν.

Τα.   ἄγε παῖ, φίλιον πρόσπτυγμα μεθεὶς
         μητρὸς μογερᾶς, βαῖνε πατρῴων
         πύργων ἐπ' ἄκρας στεφάνας, ὅθι σοι
         πνεῦμα μεθεῖναι ψῆφος ἐκράνθη.   785
         λαμβάνετ' αὐτόν. τὰ δὲ τοιάδε χρὴ
         κηρυκεύειν, ὅστις ἄνοικτος
         καὶ ἀναιδείᾳ τῆς ἡμετέρας
         γνώμης μᾶλλον φίλος ἐστίν.

Lines 790–859. Talthybius leads Andromache back to the chariot.
     Hecuba, overcome with grief that Astyanax has been taken to
     his doom, can say only: 'My cup is full, what more could
     brim it?' At this most tragic moment the women relieve
     their feelings by singing in chorus a poem describing the early
     history of Troy in its past glory. But this grandeur did not
     last. Telamon, 'king of bee-haunted Salamis,' led an
     expedition along with Heracles and destroyed the city. 'With
     the red breath of fire he blasted these walls that Apollo had
     built.' Neither its princes nor the Gods could save the city.
     This was the first sack of Troy. 'In this her hour of need,
     Troy had lost the charm that made gods love her.'

Lines 860–950. Menelaus enters, confident in his decision to
     punish Helen by death, in vengeance for all the Greeks who
     have died at Troy. He sends for her. Hecuba utters a strange
     prayer to Zeus, the god of justice, and urges Menelaus to kill
     his wife. Helen is dragged in and immediately begins to
     employ her charm and to excuse herself, blaming Menelaus
     instead for leaving her in Sparta without his protection. She
     says the real fault is Aphrodite's.

ΜΕΝΕΛΑΟΣ

 ὦ καλλιφεγγὲς ἡλίου σέλας τόδε,   860
ἐν ᾧ δάμαρτα τὴν ἐμὴν χειρώσομαι
†Ἑλένην· ὁ γὰρ δὴ πολλὰ μοχθήσας ἐγὼ
Μενέλαός εἰμι καὶ στράτευμ' Ἀχαιϊκόν.†
ἦλθον δὲ Τροίαν οὐχ ὅσον δοκοῦσί με
γυναικὸς οὕνεκ', ἀλλ' ἐπ' ἄνδρ' ὃς ἐξ ἐμῶν   865
δόμων δάμαρτα ξεναπάτης ἐλήσατο.
κεῖνος μὲν οὖν δέδωκε σὺν θεοῖς δίκην
αὐτός τε καὶ γῆ δορὶ πεσοῦσ' Ἑλληνικῷ.
ἥκω δὲ τὴν τάλαιναν—οὐ γὰρ ἡδέως
ὄνομα δάμαρτος ἥ ποτ' ἦν ἐμὴ λέγω—   870
ἄξων· δόμοις γὰρ τοῖσδ' ἐν αἰχμαλωτικοῖς
κατηρίθμηται Τρῳάδων ἄλλων μέτα.
οἵπερ γὰρ αὐτὴν ἐξεμόχθησαν δορί,
κτανεῖν ἐμοί νιν ἔδοσαν, εἴτε μὴ κτανὼν
θέλοιμ' ἄγεσθαι πάλιν ἐς Ἀργείαν χθόνα.   875
ἐμοὶ δ' ἔδοξε τὸν μὲν ἐν Τροίᾳ μόρον
Ἑλένης ἐᾶσαι, ναυπόρῳ δ' ἄγειν πλάτῃ
Ἑλληνίδ' ἐς γῆν κᾆτ' ἐκεῖ δοῦναι κτανεῖν,
ποινὰς ὅσοις τέθνασ' ἐν Ἰλίῳ φίλοι.
 ἀλλ' εἶα χωρεῖτ' ἐς δόμους, ὀπάονες,   880
κομίζετ' αὐτὴν τῆς μιαιφονωτάτης
κόμης ἐπισπάσαντες· οὔριοι δ' ὅταν
πνοαὶ μόλωσι, πέμψομέν νιν Ἑλλάδα.

Εκ. ὦ γῆς ὄχημα κἀπὶ γῆς ἔχων ἔδραν,
ὅστις ποτ' εἶ σύ, δυστόπαστος εἰδέναι,   885
Ζεύς, εἴτ' ἀνάγκη φύσεος εἴτε νοῦς βροτῶν,
προσηυξάμην σε· πάντα γὰρ δι' ἀψόφου
βαίνων κελεύθου κατὰ δίκην τὰ θνήτ' ἄγεις.
Με. τί δ' ἔστιν; εὐχὰς ὡς ἐκαίνισας θεῶν.
Εκ. αἰνῶ σε, Μενέλα', εἰ κτενεῖς δάμαρτα σήν.   890

ὁρᾶν δὲ τήνδε φεῦγε, μή σ' ἕλῃ πόθῳ.
αἱρεῖ γὰρ ἀνδρῶν ὄμματ', ἐξαιρεῖ πόλεις,
πίμπρησιν οἴκους· ὧδ' ἔχει κηλήματα.
ἐγώ νιν οἶδα, καὶ σύ, χοἱ πεπονθότες.

ΕΛΕΝΗ

   Μενέλαε, φροίμιον μὲν ἄξιον φόβου   895
τόδ' ἐστίν· ἐν γὰρ χερσὶ προσπόλων σέθεν
βίᾳ πρὸ τῶνδε δωμάτων ἐκπέμπομαι.
ἀτὰρ σχεδὸν μὲν οἶδά σοι μισουμένη,
ὅμως δ' ἐρέσθαι βούλομαι· γνῶμαι τίνες
Ἕλλησι καὶ σοὶ τῆς ἐμῆς ψυχῆς πέρι;   900

Με. οὐκ εἰς ἀκριβὲς ἦλθες, ἀλλ' ἅπας στρατὸς
κτανεῖν ἐμοί σ' ἔδωκεν, ὅνπερ ἠδίκεις.

Ελ. ἔξεστιν οὖν πρὸς ταῦτ' ἀμείψασθαι λόγῳ,
ὡς οὐ δικαίως, ἢν θάνω, θανούμεθα;

Με. οὐκ ἐς λόγους ἐλήλυθ', ἀλλά σε κτενῶν.   905

Εκ. ἄκουσον αὐτῆς, μὴ θάνῃ τοῦδ' ἐνδεής,
Μενέλαε, καὶ δὸς τοὺς ἐναντίους λόγους
ἡμῖν κατ' αὐτῆς· τῶν γὰρ ἐν Τροίᾳ κακῶν
οὐδὲν κάτοισθα. συντεθεὶς δ' ὁ πᾶς λόγος
κτενεῖ νιν οὕτως ὥστε μηδαμοῦ φυγεῖν.   910

Με σχολῆς τὸ δῶρον· εἰ δὲ βούλεται λέγειν,
ἔξεστι. τῶν σῶν δ' οὕνεχ'—ὡς μάθῃ—λόγων
δώσω τόδ' αὐτῇ· τῆσδε δ' οὐ δώσω χάριν.

Ελ. ἴσως με, κἂν εὖ κἂν κακῶς δόξω λέγειν,
οὐκ ἀνταμείψῃ πολεμίαν ἡγούμενος.   915
ἐγὼ δ', ἅ σ' οἶμαι διὰ λόγων ἰόντ' ἐμοῦ
κατηγορήσειν, ἀντιθεῖσ' ἀμείψομαι
τοῖς σοῖσι τἀμὰ καὶ τὰ σ' αἰτιάματα.
   πρῶτον μὲν ἀρχὰς ἔτεκεν ἥδε τῶν κακῶν,
Πάριν τεκοῦσα· δεύτερον δ' ἀπώλεσε   920

Τροίαν τε κἄμ᾽ ὁ πρέσβυς οὐ κτανὼν βρέφος,
δαλοῦ πικρὸν μίμημ᾽, Ἀλέξανδρόν ποτε.
ἐνθένδε τἀπίλοιπ᾽ ἄκουσον ὡς ἔχει.
ἔκρινε τρισσὸν ζεῦγος ὅδε τριῶν θεῶν
καὶ Παλλάδος μὲν ἦν Ἀλεξάνδρῳ δόσις   925
Φρυξὶ στρατηγοῦνθ᾽ Ἑλλάδ᾽ ἐξανιστάναι,
Ἥρα δ᾽ ὑπέσχετ᾽ Ἀσιάδ᾽ Εὐρώπης θ᾽ ὅρους
τυραννίδ᾽ ἕξειν, εἴ σφε κρίνειεν Πάρις·
Κύπρις δὲ τοὐμὸν εἶδος ἐκπαγλουμένη
δώσειν ὑπέσχετ᾽, εἰ θεὰς ὑπερδράμοι   930
κάλλει.   τὸν ἔνθεν δ᾽ ὡς ἔχει σκέψαι λόγον·
νικᾷ Κύπρις θεάς, καὶ τοσόνδ᾽ οὑμοὶ γάμοι
ὤνησαν Ἑλλάδ᾽· οὐ κρατεῖσθ᾽ ἐκ βαρβάρων,
οὔτ᾽ ἐς δόρυ σταθέντες, οὐ τυραννίδι.
ἃ δ᾽ εὐτύχησεν Ἑλλάς, ὠλόμην ἐγὼ   935
εὐμορφίᾳ πραθεῖσα, κὠνειδίζομαι
ἐξ ὧν ἐχρῆν με στέφανον ἐπὶ κάρᾳ λαβεῖν.
   οὔπω με φήσεις αὐτὰ τἀν ποσὶν λέγειν,
ὅπως ἀφώρμησ᾽ ἐκ δόμων τῶν σῶν λάθρα.
ἦλθ᾽ οὐχὶ μικρὰν θεὸν ἔχων αὑτοῦ μέτα   940
ὁ τῆσδ᾽ ἀλάστωρ, εἴτ᾽ Ἀλέξανδρον θέλεις
ὀνόματι προσφωνεῖν νιν εἴτε καὶ Πάριν·
ὅν, ὦ κάκιστε, σοῖσιν ἐν δόμοις λιπὼν
Σπάρτης ἀπῆρας νηὶ Κρησίαν χθόνα.
εἶεν.
οὐ σέ, ἀλλ᾽ ἐμαυτὴν τοὐπὶ τῷδ᾽ ἐρήσομαι·   945
τί δὴ φρονοῦσά γ᾽ ἐκ δόμων ἅμ᾽ ἑσπόμην
ξένῳ, προδοῦσα πατρίδα καὶ δόμους ἐμούς;
τὴν θεὸν κόλαζε καὶ Διὸς κρείσσων γενοῦ,
ὃς τῶν μὲν ἄλλων δαιμόνων ἔχει κράτος,
κείνης δὲ δοῦλός ἐστι· συγγνώμη   δ᾽ ἐμοί.   950

Lines 951–960. *Helen excuses herself for not having returned to*

*Greece when Paris was killed. She says she wanted to, and
tried to escape with a rope from the battlements.
Lines 961–1001. Helen pleads that she is excused because Paris
took her by force. Hecuba pours scorn on all Helen's excuses.*

ΕΛΕΝΗ

πῶς οὖν ἔτ᾽ ἂν θνῄσκοιμ᾽ ἂν ἐνδίκως, πόσι,

. . . .

πρὸς σοῦ δικαίως, ἢν ὁ μὲν βίᾳ γαμεῖ,
τὰ δ᾽ οἴκοθεν κεῖν᾽ ἀντὶ νικητηρίων
πικρῶς ἐδούλευσ᾽· εἰ δὲ τῶν θεῶν κρατεῖν
βούλῃ, τὸ χρῄζειν ἀμαθές ἐστί σου τόδε.   965

Χο. βασίλει᾽, ἄμυνον σοῖς τέκνοισι καὶ πάτρᾳ
πειθὼ διαφθείρουσα τῆσδ᾽, ἐπεὶ λέγει
καλῶς κακοῦργος οὖσα· δεινὸν οὖν τόδε.

Εκ. ταῖς θεαῖσι πρῶτα σύμμαχος γενήσομαι
καὶ τήνδε δείξω μὴ λέγουσαν ἔνδικα.   970
ἐγὼ γὰρ Ἥραν παρθένον τε Παλλάδα
οὐκ ἐς τοσοῦτον ἀμαθίας ἐλθεῖν δοκῶ,
ὥσθ᾽ ἡ μὲν Ἄργος βαρβάροις ἀπημπόλα,
Παλλὰς δ᾽ Ἀθήνας Φρυξὶ δουλεύειν ποτέ,
εἰ παιδιαῖσι καὶ χλιδῇ μορφῆς πέρι   975
ἦλθον πρὸς Ἴδην. τοῦ γὰρ οὕνεκ᾽ ἂν θεὰ
Ἥρα τοσοῦτον ἔσχ᾽ ἔρωτα καλλονῆς;
πότερον ἀμείνον᾽ ὡς λάβῃ Διὸς πόσιν;
ἢ γάμον Ἀθηνᾶ θεῶν τίνος θηρωμένη—
ἢ παρθενείαν πατρὸς ἐξῃτήσατο,   980
φεύγουσα λέκτρα; μὴ ἀμαθεῖς ποίει θεὰς
τὸ σὸν κακὸν κοσμοῦσα, μὴ οὐ πείσῃς σοφούς.
Κύπριν δ᾽ ἔλεξας—ταῦτα γὰρ γέλως πολύς—
ἐλθεῖν ἐμῷ ξὺν παιδὶ Μενέλεω δόμους.
οὐκ ἂν μένουσ᾽ ἂν ἥσυχός σ᾽ ἐν οὐρανῷ   985
αὐταῖς Ἀμύκλαις ἤγαγεν πρὸς Ἴλιον;

ἦν οὑμὸς υἱὸς κάλλος ἐκπρεπέστατος,
ὁ σὸς δ' ἰδών νιν νοῦς ἐποιήθη Κύπρις·
τὰ μῶρα γὰρ πάντ' ἐστὶν Ἀφροδίτη βροτοῖς,
καὶ τοὔνομ' ὀρθῶς ἀφροσύνης ἄρχει θεᾶς.   990
ὃν εἰσιδοῦσα βαρβάροις ἐσθήμασι
χρυσῷ τε λαμπρὸν ἐξεμαργώθης φρένας.
ἐν μὲν γὰρ Ἄργει μίκρ' ἔχουσ' ἀνεστρέφου,
Σπάρτης δ' ἀπαλλαχθεῖσα τὴν Φρυγῶν πόλιν
χρυσῷ ῥέουσαν ἤλπισας κατακλύσειν   995
δαπάναισιν· οὐδ' ἦν ἱκανά σοι τὰ Μενέλεω
μέλαθρα ταῖς σαῖς ἐγκαθυβρίζειν τρυφαῖς.

εἶέν· βίᾳ γὰρ παῖδα φῄς ⟨σ'⟩ ἄγειν ἐμόν·
τίς Σπαρτιατῶν ᾔσθετ'; ἢ ποίαν βοὴν
ἀνωλόλυξας—Κάστορος νεανίου   1000
τοῦ συζύγου τ' ἔτ' ὄντος, οὐ κατ' ἄστρα πω;

Lines 1002–1019. *Hecuba now accuses Helen of duplicity in
supporting whichever side was winning, and denies her claim
to have attempted to escape. She says she had offered to
smuggle her back to Greece to stop the war, but Helen would
not hear of this.*

Lines 1020–1059. *Hecuba taunts Helen with the frivolity and
selfishness of her life in Troy. The Chorus join her in urging
Menelaus to inflict the death-penalty on his adulterous wife.
He tells Helen that she is to be stoned to death; but her death
is to be postponed until they reach Sparta.*

ΕΚΑΒΗ

ἐν τοῖς Ἀλεξάνδρου γὰρ ὕβριζες δόμοις   1020
καί προσκυνεῖσθαι βαρβάρων ὕπ' ἤθελες·
μεγάλα γὰρ ἦν σοι.—κἀπὶ τοῖσδε σὸν δέμας
ἐξῆλθες ἀσκήσασα κἄβλεψας πόσει
τὸν αὐτὸν αἰθέρ', ὦ κατάπτυστον κάρα·
ἦν χρῆν ταπεινὴν ἐν πέπλων ἐρειπίοις,   1025

φρίκῃ τρέμουσαν, κρᾶτ' ἀπεσκυθισμένην
ἐλθεῖν, τὸ σῶφρον τῆς ἀναιδείας πλέον
ἔχουσαν ἐπὶ τοῖς πρόσθεν ἡμαρτημένοις.

   Μενέλα', ἵν' εἰδῇς οἷ τελευτήσω λόγον,
στεφάνωσον Ἑλλάδ' ἀξίως τήνδε κτανὼν   1030
σαυτοῦ, νόμον δὲ τόνδε ταῖς ἄλλαισι θὲς
γυναιξί, θνήσκειν ἥτις ἂν προδῷ πόσιν.

Χο. Μενέλαε, προγόνων τ' ἀξίως δόμων τε σῶν
τεῖσαι δάμαρτα κἀφελοῦ, πρὸς Ἑλλάδος,
ψόγον τὸ θῆλύ τ', εὐγενὴς ἐχθροῖς φανείς.   1035

Με. ἐμοὶ σὺ συμπέπτωκας ἐς ταὐτὸν λόγου,
ἑκουσίως τήνδ' ἐκ δόμων ἐλθεῖν ἐμῶν
ξένας ἐς εὐνάς· χἠ Κύπρις κόμπου χάριν
λόγοις ἐνεῖται.—βαῖνε λευστήρων πέλας
πόνους τ' Ἀχαιῶν ἀπόδος ἐν μικρῷ μακροὺς   1040
θανοῦσ', ἵν' εἰδῇς μὴ καταισχύνειν ἐμέ.

Ἑλ. μή, προς σε γονάτων, τὴν νόσον τὴν τῶν θεῶν
προσθεὶς ἐμοὶ κτάνῃς με, συγγίγνωσκε δέ.

Ἑκ. μηδ' οὓς ἀπέκτειν' ἥδε συμμάχους προδῷς·
ἐγὼ πρὸ κείνων καὶ τέκνων σε λίσσομαι.   1045

Με. παῦσαι, γεραιά· τῆσδε δ' οὐκ ἐφρόντισα.
λέγω δὲ προσπόλοισι πρὸς πρύμνας νεῶν
τήνδ' ἐκκομίζειν, ἔνθα ναυστολήσεται.

Ἑκ. μή νυν νεὼς σοὶ ταὐτὸν ἐσβήτω σκάφος.

Με. τί δ' ἔστι; μεῖζον βρῖθος ἢ πάροιθ' ἔχει;   1050

Ἑκ. οὐκ ἔστ' ἐραστὴς ὅστις οὐκ ἀεὶ φιλεῖ.

Με. ὅπως ἂν ἐκβῇ τῶν ἐρωμένων ὁ νοῦς.
ἔσται δ' ἃ βούλῃ· ναῦν γὰρ οὐκ ἐσβήσεται
ἐς ἥνπερ ἡμεῖς· καὶ γὰρ οὐ κακῶς λέγεις·
ἐλθοῦσα δ' Ἄργος ὥσπερ ἀξία κακῶς   1055
κακὴ θανεῖται καὶ γυναιξὶ σωφρονεῖν
πάσαισι θήσει. ῥᾴδιον μὲν οὐ τόδε·

D

ὅμως δ' ὁ τῆσδ' ὄλεθρος ἐς φόβον βαλεῖ
τὸ μῶρον αὐτῶν, κἂν ἔτ' ὦσ' ἐχθίονες.

*Lines 1060–1122. Menelaus goes out, pleased with himself. The
women, again in a choral ode, return to the theme of the
abandonment of Troy by the gods, and the waste of the many
sacrifices made to them. The younger women and girls chant
farewells to their absent mothers, and curse Menelaus and
Helen, who ' plays with her golden mirrors and those light
luxuries that all brides love '. They pray that he may never
reach his Spartan home, but that Zeus may send ' a blazing
Aegean thunderbolt to crash upon his slave-ship '.*

> *News comes that Astyanax has been hurled from the
> battlements. Talthybius enters. His men carry Hector's
> shield, which holds the child's body.*

*Lines 1123–1193. Talthybius tells Hecuba that Andromache has
been hurried away on board Pyrrhus's ship. He himself
brings the body of Astyanax: Andromache had no time to
bury it, but asked that her son should be buried in Hector's
shield for a coffin. Talthybius and his men go out to dig the
grave, and Hecuba is left to mourn over her dead grandson
and to recall the pleasure she had in him.*

Τα. Ἑκάβη, νεὼς μὲν πίτυλος εἷς λελειμμένος
    λάφυρα τἀπίλοιπ' Ἀχιλλείου τόκου
    μέλλει πρὸς ἀκτὰς ναυστολεῖν Φθιώτιδας·   1125
    αὐτὸς δ' ἀνῆκται Νεοπτόλεμος, καινάς τινας
    Πηλέως ἀκούσας συμφοράς, ὥς νιν χθονὸς
    Ἄκαστος ἐκβέβληκεν, ὁ Πελίου γόνος.
    οὗ θᾶσσον οὕνεκ', ἢ χάριν μονῆς ἔχων,
    φροῦδος, μετ' αὐτοῦ δ' Ἀνδρομάχη, πολλῶν ἐμοὶ   1130
    δακρύων ἀγωγός, ἡνίκ' ἐξώρμα χθονός,
    πάτραν τ' ἀναστένουσα καὶ τὸν Ἕκτορος
    τύμβον προσεννέπουσα. καί σφ' ᾐτήσατο
    θάψαι νεκρὸν τόνδ', ὃς πεσὼν ἐκ τειχέων

ψυχὴν ἀφῆκεν Ἕκτορος τοῦ σοῦ γόνος·   1135
φόβον τ᾽ Ἀχαιῶν, χαλκόνωτον ἀσπίδα
τήνδ᾽, ἣν πατὴρ τοῦδ᾽ ἀμφὶ πλεύρ᾽ ἐβάλλετο,
μή νυν πορεῦσαι Πηλέως ἐφ᾽ ἑστίαν,
μηδ᾽ ἐς τὸν αὐτὸν θάλαμον, οὗ νυμφεύσεται
μήτηρ νεκροῦ τοῦδ᾽ Ἀνδρομάχη, λύπας ὁρᾶν,   1140
ἀλλ᾽ ἀντὶ κέδρου περιβόλων τε λαΐνων
ἐν τῇδε θάψαι παῖδα· σὰς δ᾽ ἐς ὠλένας
δοῦναι, πέπλοισιν ὡς περιστείλῃς νεκρὸν
στεφάνοις θ᾽, ὅση σοι δύναμις, ὡς ἔχει τὰ σά·
ἐπεὶ βέβηκε, καὶ τὸ δεσπότου τάχος   1145
ἀφείλετ᾽ αὐτὴν παῖδα μὴ δοῦναι τάφῳ.

    ἡμεῖς μὲν οὖν, ὅταν σὺ κοσμήσῃς νέκυν,
γῆν τῷδ᾽ ἐπαμπισχόντες ἀροῦμεν δόρυ·
σὺ δ᾽ ὡς τάχιστα πρᾶσσε τἀπεσταλμένα.

    ἑνὸς μὲν οὖν μόχθου σ᾽ ἀπαλλάξας ἔχω·   1150
Σκαμανδρίους γὰρ τάσδε διαπερῶν ῥοὰς
ἔλουσα νεκρὸν κἀπένιψα τραύματα.

    ἀλλ᾽ εἶμ᾽ ὀρυκτὸν τῷδ᾽ ἀναρρήξων τάφον,
ὡς σύντομ᾽ ἡμῖν τἀπ᾽ ἐμοῦ τε κἀπὸ σοῦ
ἐς ἓν ξυνελθόντ᾽ οἴκαδ᾽ ὁρμήσῃ πλάτην.   1155

Εκ. θέσθ᾽ ἀμφίτορνον ἀσπίδ᾽ Ἕκτορος πέδῳ,
λυπρὸν θέαμα κοὐ φίλον λεύσσειν ἐμοί.

    ὦ μεῖζον᾽ ὄγκον δορὸς ἔχοντες ἢ φρενῶν,
τί τόνδ᾽, Ἀχαιοί, παῖδα δείσαντες φόνον
καινὸν διειργάσασθε; μὴ Τροίαν ποτὲ   1160
πεσοῦσαν ὀρθώσειεν; οὐδὲν ἦτ᾽ ἄρα,
ὅθ᾽ Ἕκτορος μὲν εὐτυχοῦντος ἐς δόρυ
διωλλύμεσθα μυρίας τ᾽ ἄλλης χερός,
πόλεως δ᾽ ἁλούσης καὶ Φρυγῶν ἐφθαρμένων
βρέφος τοσόνδ᾽ ἐδείσατ᾽· οὐκ αἰνῶ φόβον,   1165

ὅστις φοβεῖται μὴ διεξελθὼν λόγῳ.
  ὦ φίλταθ᾽, ὥς σοι θάνατος ἦλθε δυστυχής.
εἰ μὲν γὰρ ἔθανες πρὸ πόλεως, ἥβης τυχὼν
γάμων τε καὶ τῆς ἰσοθέου τυραννίδος,
μακάριος ἦσθ᾽ ἄν, εἴ τι τῶνδε μακάριον· 1170
νῦν δ᾽ αὖτ᾽ ἰδὼν μὲν γνούς τε σῇ ψυχῇ, τέκνον,
οὐκ οἶσθ᾽, ἐχρήσω δ᾽ οὐδὲν ἐν δόμοις ἔχων.
δύστηνε, κρατὸς ὥς σ᾽ ἔκειρεν ἀθλίως
τείχη πατρῷα, Λοξίου πυργώματα,
ὃν πόλλ᾽ ἐκήπευσ᾽ ἡ τεκοῦσα βόστρυχον 1175
φιλήμασίν τ᾽ ἔδωκεν, ἔνθεν ἐκγελᾷ
ὀστέων ῥαγέντων φόνος, ἵν᾽ αἰσχρὰ μὴ λέγω.
ὦ χεῖρες, ὡς εἰκοὺς μὲν ἡδείας πατρὸς
κέκτησθ᾽, ἐν ἄρθροις δ᾽ ἔκλυτοι πρόκεισθέ μοι.
ὦ πολλὰ κόμπους ἐκβαλὸν φίλον στόμα, 1180
ὄλωλας, ἐψεύσω μ᾽, ὅτ᾽ ἐσπίπτων πέπλους,
᾿Ω μῆτερ, ηὔδας, ἦ πολύν σοι βοστρύχων
πλόκαμον κεροῦμαι, πρὸς τάφον θ᾽ ὁμηλίκων
κώμους ἀπάξω, φίλα διδοὺς προσφθέγματα.
σὺ δ᾽ οὐκ ἔμ᾽, ἀλλ᾽ ἐγὼ σὲ τὸν νεώτερον, 1185
γραῦς ἄπολις ἄτεκνος, ἄθλιον θάπτω νεκρόν.
οἴμοι, τὰ πόλλ᾽ ἀσπάσμαθ᾽ αἵ τ᾽ ἐμαὶ τροφαὶ
ὕπνοι τ᾽ ἐκεῖνοι φροῦδά μοι. τί καί ποτε
γράψειεν ἄν σε μουσοποιὸς ἐν τάφῳ;
Τὸν παῖδα τόνδ᾽ ἔκτειναν ᾿Αργεῖοί ποτε 1190
δείσαντες;—αἰσχρὸν τοὐπίγραμμά γ᾽ ῾Ελλάδι.
ἀλλ᾽ οὖν πατρῴων οὐ λαχὼν ἕξεις ὅμως
ἐν ᾗ ταφήσῃ χαλκόνωτον ἰτέαν.

Lines 1194–1199. *Hecuba addresses the shield which protected
Hector for so long and still bears imprints of his hands; then
she turns to the women.*

Lines 1200–1286. With the help of the Chorus, Hecuba prepares
the corpse for burial, and they mourn together. Talthybius
returns and orders his men to fire the citadel. He tells
Hecuba and the other women that when the trumpet sounds
they are to go on board. Hecuba tries to throw herself into the
flames.

ΕΚΑΒΗ

φέρετε, κομίζετ' ἀθλίῳ κόσμον νεκρῷ   1200
ἐκ τῶν παρόντων· οὐ γὰρ ἐς κάλλος τύχας
δαίμων δίδωσιν· ὧν δ' ἔχω, λήψῃ τάδε.
    θνητῶν δὲ μῶρος ὅστις εὖ πράσσειν δοκῶν
βέβαια χαίρει· τοῖς τρόποις γὰρ αἱ τύχαι,
ἔμπληκτος ὡς ἄνθρωπος, ἄλλοτ' ἄλλοσε   1205
πηδῶσι, κοὐδεὶς αὐτὸς εὐτυχεῖ ποτε.

Χο. καὶ μὴν πρόχειρον αἵδε σοι σκυλευμάτων
    Φρυγίων φέρουσι κόσμον ἐξάπτειν νεκρῷ.

Εκ. ὦ τέκνον, οὐχ ἵπποισι νικήσαντά σε
    οὐδ' ἥλικας τόξοισιν, οὓς Φρύγες νόμους   1210
    τιμῶσιν, οὐκ ἐς πλησμονὰς θηρωμένη,
    μήτηρ πατρός σοι προστίθησ' ἀγάλματα
    τῶν σῶν ποτ' ὄντων· νῦν δέ σ' ἡ θεοστυγὴς
    ἀφείλεθ' Ἑλένη, πρὸς δὲ καὶ ψυχὴν σέθεν
    ἔκτεινε καὶ πάντ' οἶκον ἐξαπώλεσεν.   1215

Χο. —   ἒ ἔ, φρενῶν
        ἔθιγες ἔθιγες· ὦ μέγας ἐμοί ποτ' ὢν
        ἀνάκτωρ πόλεως.

Εκ. ἃ δ' ἐν γάμοισι χρῆν σε προσθέσθαι χροΐ
    Ἀσιατίδων γήμαντα τὴν ὑπερτάτην,
    Φρύγια πέπλων ἀγάλματ' ἐξάπτω χροός.   1220
    σύ τ', ὦ ποτ' οὖσα καλλίνικε, μυρίων
    μῆτερ τροπαίων, Ἕκτορος φίλον σάκος,

στεφανοῦ· θάνῃ γὰρ οὐ θανοῦσα σὺν νεκρῷ·
ἐπεὶ σὲ πολλῷ μᾶλλον ἢ τὰ τοῦ σοφοῦ
κακοῦ τ᾽ Ὀδυσσέως ἄξιον τιμᾶν ὅπλα.   1225

Χο. —   αἰαῖ αἰαῖ· πικρὸν ὄδυρμα . . .
    —   γαῖά σ᾽ ὦ τέκνον δέξεται.
    —   στέναζε, μᾶτερ,   Εκ. αἰαῖ.
Χο. —   νεκρῶν ἴακχον.   Εκ. οἴμοι [μοι].   1230
Χο. —   οἴμοι δῆτα σῶν ἀλάστων κακῶν.
Εκ. τελαμῶσιν ἕλκη τὰ μὲν ἐγώ σ᾽ ἰάσομαι,
τλήμων ἰατρός, ὄνομ᾽ ἔχουσα, τἄργα δ᾽ οὔ·
τὰ δ᾽ ἐν νεκροῖσι φροντιεῖ πατὴρ σέθεν.
Χο. —   ἄρασσ᾽ ἄρασσε κρᾶτα   1235
    πιτύλους διδοῦσα χειρός,
    ἰώ μοί μοι.
Εκ.   ὦ φίλταται γυναῖκες . . .
Χο. —   Ἑκάβη, σὰς ἔνεπε· τίνα θροεῖς αὐδάν;
Εκ. οὐκ ἦν ἄρ᾽ ἐν θεοῖσι πλὴν οὑμοὶ πόνοι   1240
Τροία τε πόλεων ἔκκριτον μισουμένη,
μάτην δ᾽ ἐβουθυτοῦμεν. εἰ δὲ μὴ θεὸς
ἔστρεψε τἄνω περιβαλὼν κάτω χθονός,
ἀφανεῖς ἂν ὄντες οὐκ ἂν ὑμνήθημεν ἂν
μούσαις ἀοιδὰς δόντες ὑστέρων βροτῶν.   1245
    χωρεῖτε, θάπτετ᾽ ἀθλίῳ τύμβῳ νεκρόν·
ἔχει γὰρ οἷα δεῖ γε νερτέρων στέφη.
δοκῶ δὲ τοῖς θανοῦσι διαφέρειν βραχύ,
εἰ πλουσίων τις τεύξεται κτερισμάτων·
κενὸν δὲ γαύρωμ᾽ ἐστὶ τῶν ζώντων τόδε.   1250

Χο. —ἰὼ ἰώ·
    μελέα μήτηρ, ἢ τὰς μεγάλας
    ἐλπίδας ἐν σοὶ κατέκναψε βίου.
    μέγα δ᾽ ὀλβισθεὶς ὡς ἐκ πατέρων

ἀγαθῶν ἐγένου,
δεινῷ θανάτῳ διόλωλας.   1255
— ἔα ἔα·
τίνας Ἰλιάσιν ταῖσδ' ἐν κορυφαῖς
λεύσσω φλογέας δαλοῖσι χέρας
διερέσσοντας; μέλλει Τροίᾳ
καινόν τι κακὸν προσέσεσθαι.

Τα. αὐδῶ λοχαγοῖς, οἳ τέταχθ' ἐμπιμπράναι   1260
Πριάμου τόδ' ἄστυ, μηκέτ' ἀργοῦσαν φλόγα
ἐν χειρὶ σῴζειν ἀλλὰ πῦρ ἐνιέναι,
ὡς ἂν κατασκάψαντες Ἰλίου πόλιν
στελλώμεθ' οἴκαδ' ἄσμενοι Τροίας ἄπο.

    ὑμεῖς δ', ἵν' αὑτὸς λόγος ἔχῃ μορφὰς δύο,   1265
χωρεῖτε, Τρώων παῖδες, ὀρθίαν ὅταν
σάλπιγγος ἠχὼ δῶσιν ἀρχηγοὶ στρατοῦ,
πρὸς ναῦς Ἀχαιῶν, ὡς ἀποστέλλησθε γῆς.

    σύ τ', ὦ γεραιὰ δυστυχεστάτη γύναι,
ἕπου. μεθήκουσίν σ' Ὀδυσσέως πάρα   1270
οἶδ', ᾧ σε δούλην κλῆρος ἐκπέμπει πάτρας.

Εκ. οἲ 'γὼ τάλαινα· τοῦτο δὴ τὸ λοίσθιον
καὶ τέρμα πάντων τῶν ἐμῶν ἤδη κακῶν·
ἔξειμι πατρίδος, πόλις ὑφάπτεται πυρί.
ἀλλ', ὦ γεραιὲ πούς, ἐπίσπευσον μόλις,   1275
ὡς ἀσπάσωμαι τὴν ταλαίπωρον πόλιν.

    ὦ μεγάλα δή ποτ' ἀμπνέουσ' ἐν βαρβάροις
Τροία, τὸ κλεινὸν ὄνομ' ἀφαιρήσῃ τάχα.
πιμπρᾶσί σ', ἡμᾶς δ' ἐξάγουσ' ἤδη χθονὸς
δούλας· ἰὼ θεοί. καὶ τί τοὺς θεοὺς καλῶ;   1280
καὶ πρὶν γὰρ οὐκ ἤκουσαν ἀνακαλούμενοι.

    φέρ' ἐς πυρὰν δράμωμεν· ὡς κάλλιστά μοι
σὺν τῇδε πατρίδι κατθανεῖν πυρουμένῃ.

Τα. ἐνθουσιᾷς, δύστηνε, τοῖς σαυτῆς κακοῖς.

ἀλλ' ἄγετε, μὴ φείδεσθ'· Ὀδυσσέως δὲ χρὴ   1285
ἐς χεῖρα δοῦναι τήνδε καὶ πέμπειν γέρας.

Lines 1287–1332. The soldiers seize Hecuba to take her away.
In desperation she appeals first to the founder of her royal
race and then, tearing at the ground, to her dead children and
her husband. ' Priam, my Priam, murdered, unburied,
friendless, you know nothing of my grief. They drive us like
cattle from our country to a slave land.'

The flames spread and the crash of falling masonry is
heard. Signs of an oncoming storm are observed. Hecuba
sees the dust, ' like billowing smoke ' blotting out her home.
The trumpet sounds from the Greek ships. The last words of
the chorus are: ' Farewell, unhappy city! To the Greek
ships. . . .' As the trumpet sounds a second time the women
go out one by one in silence.

NOTES

Line 1. λιπών, see λείπω. Αἴγαιον. The Aegean sea is between Greece and Asia.

l.2. Νηρήδων for Νηρηίδων. The Nereids were sea-nymphs, daughters of Nereus.

l.3. κάλλιστος, superlative of καλός .

l.4. ἐξ οὗ, from the time when. τήνδε would in prose be followed by τήν. In tragedy the demonstrative is frequently used without the article.

l.5. Φοῖβος, Phoebus Apollo; see Introduction, 3. κἀγώ, καὶ ἐγώ. λαΐνους (3 syllables), adj. from λᾶας, stone.

l.6. (The second foot is a tribrach and the third a dactyl.) ἔθεμεν, see τίθημι. κανόσιν, see κανών. οὔποτ᾽, οὔποτε. φρενῶν, see φρήν.

l.7. εὔνοι᾽, εὔνοια. ἀπέστη, see ἀφίστημι. Φρυγῶν, genitive, depending on πόλει: from Φρύξ, Phrygian; it often means Trojan. πόλει dative, with εὔνοια: goodwill towards the city.

l.8. πρός with genitive indicates origin of a thing, action or state. ᾽Αργείου, adj. from ῎Αργος : Argive, or simply Greek.

l.9. ὄλωλε, see ὄλλυμι. πορθηθεῖσα, from πορθέω, equiv. to πέρθω, destroy, ravage.

ll.9–10. ῾Ο Παρνάσιος Φωκεύς ᾽Επειός. Epeius came from Phocis, the district of Greece where Mt. Parnassus stands. Παλλάδος, of Pallas (Athena); see Introduction, 3.

l.11. τευχέων, gen. depending on ἐγκύμονα.

l.12. (The 4th foot is a tribrach.) πύργων, gen. depending on ἐντός.

ll.13–14. The square brackets show that some scholars believe that Euripides did not write the enclosed passage.

l.13. ἀνδρῶν, see ἀνήρ. κεκλήσεται, fut. perf. passive of καλέω. πρός, see l.8, note; here equiv. to ὑπό.

l.14. Δούρειος, adj. connected with δόρυ: it has more than one meaning, as δόρυ means a beam, mast, plank, or the shaft of a spear and hence the spear itself. ἀμπισχών, aorist participle of ἀμπέχω, enclose. δόρυ, sing. for pl.

l.16. πρός with dative (βάθροις), at, near.

l.17. πέπτωκε, see πίπτω. Πρίαμος, see Introduction, 3. Ζηνός, genitive of Ζεύς. (In prose, gen. is usually Διός.) θανών, see θνήσκω.

l.18. (The 3rd foot is a dactyl.) Φρύγια, Phrygian; see 7, note.

l.19. πρός with accusative (ναῦς, acc. pl.), to. 'Αχαιῶν, Achaean, like Argive; see 8, note. μένουσι, subject, the Greeks.

l.20. πρύμνηθεν, adverb used as adjective with οὖρον, from the stern. ὡς, equivalent to ἵνα. δεκασπόρῳ χρόνῳ, in a period of ten seed-times (springs).

l.21. (The 1st foot is an anapaest.) εἰσίδωσιν, see εἰσοράω.

l.23. νικῶμαι, understand ὑπὸ 'Αργείας θεοῦ. But this gen. is like the gen. of comparison with ἥσσων and ἡσσάομαι. θεοῦ. θεός is fem. as well as masc., although θεά is also found.

l.24. "Ηρας, see Introduction, 3. 'Αθάνας, Doric form of 'Αθήνης. θ', τέ, aspirated because αἱ follows. συνεξεῖλον, see συνεξαιρέω.

l.25. τὸ "Ιλιον in Tragedy, but ἡ "Ιλιος in Homer.

l.26. (The 2nd foot is an anapaest.) λάβῃ, see λαμβάνω.

l.27. (θεῶν, here, as often, a monosyllable.) τιμᾶσθαι θέλει, equiv. to a future; cf. English auxiliary will.

l.28. πολλοῖς, see πολύς.

l.29. βοᾷ, re-echoes. Σκάμανδρος, Scamander, the river of Troy.

l.30. 'Αρκάς, nom. sing., Arcadian. Arcadia and Thessaly represent the south and north of Greece.

l.31. εἴληχε, see λαγχάνω. Θησεῖδαι, descendants of Theseus, the famous king of Athens; i.e. Acamas and Demophon.

l.32. ἄκληροι, chosen without the drawing of lots.

l.33. ἐξῃρημέναι, see ἐξαιρέω.

l.34. ἡ Λάκαινα Τυνδαρίς, the Spartan daughter of Tyndareus.

l.35. (The 1st foot is an anapaest.) αἰχμάλωτος, masc. and fem. alike, although in l. 28 the 3rd declension fem. noun αἰχμαλωτίς is used.

l.36. τήνδε. Poseidon indicates Hecuba by glance or gesture.

l.37. (The 2nd foot is a tribrach.) πυλῶν πάρος, πρὸ πυλῶν.

l.38. (The 1st foot is an anapaest.) ὕπερ, thus accented as it follows its noun.

l.38. Ἀχιλλείου, adj., of Achilles; see Introduction, 3.

l.40. Πολυξένη. See Introduction, 3.

l.41. (The 2nd foot is a tribrach.) φροῦδος, agrees with Πρίαμος, the first part of a compound subject. παρθένον, predicative.

l.42. (The 3rd foot is a dactyl.) μεθῆκε, see μεθίημι. Κασάνδραν, see Introduction, 3. Apollo loved her, but when she refused him he punished her with madness.

l.43. (The 3rd foot is a tribrach.) παραλιπών, see παραλείπω.

l.44. (The 3rd foot is a dactyl and the 4th a tribrach.) γαμεῖ, probably present, not future. σκότιον λέχος, as an unlawful wife. Ἀγαμέμνων, king of Mycenae, brother of Menelaus and commander-in-chief of the Greek expedition against Troy.

l.45. μοι, ' I say '.

l.46. διώλεσεν, see διόλλυμι.

l.47. Παλλὰς Διὸς παῖς, see ll. 10 and 17, notes. ἦσθ' ἂν . . . ἔτι, you would still be.

l.48. Here, as often, there is no interrogative particle. ' Is it permitted for me, having put an end to my former enmity, to address . . . ? ' ἄγχιστον, superlative adj. from adverb ἄγχι, near; it governs the gen., πατρός.

l.50. λύσασαν, referring to herself. (ἔξεστι usually takes dative, not acc.)

l.52. ἄνασσα, fem. of ἄναξ. φίλτρον, complement, without a verb.

l.53. ἐπῄνεσα, see ἐπαινέω: aorist, to be translated ' I at once approve '.

l.54. ἐμαυτῇ τε, equiv. to καὶ ἐμαυτῇ.

l.55. (θεῶν is here 2 syllables.) μῶν, interrog. particle, equiv. to ἆρα μή. του, enclitic, equiv. to τινός in 56. θεῶν is partitive, depending on του.

l.56. πάρα, see note on ὕπερ, 38.

l.57. βαίνομεν, ' we set our feet '; it does not necessarily mean that they are walking about.

l.58. (The 3rd foot is a dactyl.) ἀφῖγμαι, see ἀφικνέομαι. ὡς, as in 20. λάβω, see 26.

l.59. ἦ, interrog. particle. πού (enclitic), somewhere. νιν, equiv. to αὐτήν (Troy). ἐκβαλοῦσα, see ἐκβάλλω.

l.60. (The 3rd foot is a dactyl.) ἐς οἶκον ἦλθες, ' you have

come to pity '; governs direct object, νιν. ἦλθες, see ἔρχομαι. κατηθαλωμένης seeκαταιθαλόω: forms gen. abs. with Τροίας, understood.

1.61. ἐκεῖσε, ' to the former point '; κοινώσῃ, middle.

1.62. ἂν, ἃ ἄν, ' whatever things ', in Indefinite Clause.

1.63. τὸ σόν. Supply a noun, such as ' wish ', ' intention '.
μαθεῖν, see μανθάνω.

1.64. (The 1st foot is a tribrach.)

1.65. Τρῶας, see Τρῶς.

1.66. ἐμβαλεῖν, see ἐμβάλλω.

1.67. ἄλλοτε εἰς ἄλλους τρόπους, ' now one way and now another '.

1.68. ὃν ἂν τύχῃς, ' at random '. See τυγχάνω.

1.69. οἶσθα, see οἶδα. ὑβρισθεῖσάν με, acc. with participle, where
Latin would have acc. with infin.

1.70. Αἴας, the Greek leader, son of Oileus. εἷλκε, see ἕλκω.

1.71. (The 3rd foot is a dactyl.) κοὐδέν, καὶ οὐδέν. Ἀχαιῶν,
depends on ὕπο. ἔπαθεν, see πάσχω. ἤκουσε, ' he was told '.
' And he suffered no punishment or reproach from the Greeks.'

1.72. ἔπερσαν, see πέρθω.

1.73. σφε, equiv. to αὐτούς, acc. depending on δρᾶσαι κακῶς, ' to
harm '.

1.74. τἀπ᾽ ἐμοῦ, τὰ ἐπὶ ἐμοῦ, ' the things under my authority '.

1.75. δύσνοστον, a verbal contradiction: ' a home-coming
which is no home-coming '.

1.76. μενόντων, gen. abs., although the dative might have been
used, agreeing with αὐτοῖς in 75. καθ᾽, before an aspirated
vowel, for κατά. (Cf. θ᾽, 25, note.) ἅλα, see ἅλς.

1.80. δώσειν, see δίδωμι.

1.81. βάλλειν, infin. of purpose after δώσειν. (The infin. was
originally a dative: ' for throwing '.) πιμπράναι, see πίμπρημι
(present system as ἵστημι).

1.82. τὸ σὸν [μέρος], ' for your part '. παράσχες, aor. imperative
act. of παρέχω.

1.84. πλῆσον, see πίμπλημι. Εὐβοίας μυχόν, that side of the
island of Euboea which faces Andros (east of Attica).

1.85. τὸ λοιπόν, ' for the future '.

1.86. εἰδῶσι, subjunctive of οἶδα.

1.89. (The 2nd foot is a tribrach.) Myconos and Delos are
about half-way across the Aegean, S.E. of Attica.

1.90. Scyros and Lemnos are further north. Caphareus is a promontory on the south coast of Euboea.

1.91. σώμαθ', σώματα, see 25 and 76, notes. θανόντων, see 17, note.

1.92. "Ολυμπον, ' to Olympus '. O. was the highest mountain in Greece, the home of the gods and of Zeus in particular.

1.93. χερῶν, see χείρ. καραδόκει, ὅταν, ' wait for the moment when '.

1.94. ἐξιῇ, see ἐξίημι. κάλως, acc. pl. of κάλως, κάλω, ὁ, cable. ἐξιέναι κάλως, to set sail.

1.96. (The 3rd foot is a dactyl.) τῶν κεκμηκότων, ' of the dead '; see κάμνω.

1.97. δούς, see δίδωμι. ὤλετο, ' gnomic ' aorist, ' has often perished '. See ὄλλυμι.

1.230. The Chorus, in lyric metre, continues. καὶ μήν attracts our attention to the entrance of the herald: ' But look! ' Δαναῶν. The Danaans were the subjects of King Danaus of Argos; often simply Greeks; cf. 8, note.

1.234. Δωρίδος, Dorian (Greek).

1.235. (The 1st foot is an anapaest.) Talthybius speaks in iambics, but Hecuba still uses lyric metre. οἶσθα . . . ἐλθόντα, see 69, note, and 60, note.

1.236. 'Αχαιικοῦ, see 19, note.

1.237. ἐγνωσμένος, perf. part. pass. of γιγνώσκω.

1.238. (The 1st foot is a dactyl.)

1.239. ⟨αἰαῖ⟩. The pointed brackets indicate that the scholar who edited the text (Gilbert Murray in this case) has guessed how to fill in a gap in the ancient manuscript.

1.239a. τόδε [ἐστί]. φόβος ἦν, equiv. to ἐφοβούμην.

1.240. κεκλήρωσθε, see κληρόω.

1.243. Φθιάδος, adj., ' of Phthia ' (south of Thessaly, the district from which Achilles came). εἶπας, see λέγω. Note that the aorist εἶπον has some strong forms and some weak. Καδμείας χθονός, ' of the land of Cadmus '; here it means not his city (Thebes) but the district of Boeotia, north of Attica.

1.244. κατ' ἄνδρ' ἑκάστη, each to a different man. λελόγχατε, see λαγχάνω: intransitive here, ' you have fallen to the lot '.

1.244a. ἔλαχε, see λαγχάνω.

l.245. Ἰλιάδων, ' of the women of Troy ' (Ilium).

l.246 πάνθ', πάντα.

l.248. τλήμονα, Doric for τλήμονα.

l.249. (The 3rd and 4th feet are tribrachs.) ἐξαίρετον, fem. νιν, αὐτήν.

l.249a. τᾷ . . . νύμφᾳ, Doric for τῇ . . . νύμφῃ. (Doric forms are often used in lyric metres in Tragedy.) Λακεδαιμονίᾳ, Spartan, refers to Clytaemnestra, sister of Helen.

l.250. δούλαν, Doric for δούλην.

l.251. (The 3rd foot is a dactyl.) λέκτρων, pl. for sing., bed.

l.252. τὰν . . . ᾷ, Doric for τὴν . . . ῇ. Φοίβου, see 42, note.

l.253. χρυσοκόμας, masc. sing. nom., ' golden-haired '. ἔδωκε, see δίδωμι. ζόαν, Doric for ζωήν.

l.256. κλῇδας, usually bolts or keys; here garlands.

l.257. χροός, gen. of χρώς, skin.

l.259. (The 3rd foot is a dactyl.) μέγα, ' a great thing '. τυχεῖν, see 68, note.

l.260. τί δ' ὃ . . . τέκος, ' and what of the child which . . . ? ' ἐμέθεν, equiv. to ἐμοῦ. ἐλάβετε, pl., ' you Greeks took '.

l.262. τῷ, interrog., τίνι. ἔζευξεν, see ζεύγνυμι.

l.264. τέτακται, see τάσσω.

l.265. ἐτεκόμαν, Doric for ἐτεκόμην, see τίκτω.

l.267. φίλος for φίλε, vocative. Ἑλλάνων, Doric for Ἑλλήνων.

l.268. ἔχει καλῶς, ' it is well with her '.

l.269. ἔλακες, aor. of λάσκω, shout, cry. ἀέλιον, Doric for ἥλιον.

l.270. ὥστε with infin. expresses result. ἀπηλλάχθαι, see ἀπαλλάσσω.

l.271. ἁ Doric for ἡ. χαλκεομήστορος, adj. in genitive, ' skilled n arms '.

l.272. Ἀνδρομάχα . . . τύχαν, Doric for Ἀνδρομάχη . . . τύχην.

l.273. (Ἀχιλλέως. The ending -έως is here one syllable; the 3rd foot is thus a dactyl.) Ἀχιλλέως παῖς, Pyrrhus Neoptolemus.

l.274. τῷ, as in 262.

l.275. ἁ, Doric for ἡ. τριτοβάμονος (genitive with βάκτρου), ' a third foot '.

l.276. δευομένα, Doric for δευομένη. κάρᾳ, neuter in spite of its form.

l.277. (The 1st foot is an anapaest, the 3rd a dactyl.)

Odysseus, king of the western island of Ithaca, had a reputation for cunning as well as courage.

1.280. ὀνύχεσσι, equiv. to ὄνυξι.   δίπτυχον παρειάν, ' either cheek '.

1.282. λέλογχα, see 244, note.   φωτί, dat. of φώς, man.

1.283. δίκας, Doric for δίκης.

1.285. ὅς, masc., referring to φωτί, not to δάκει.   τἀκεῖθεν, τὰ ἐκεῖθεν.   ἐνθάδε, predicative, as ἄφιλα, 287.

1.286. γλώσσᾳ, Doric for γλώσσῃ.

ll.285–287. Trans: ' who reverses all things, setting here what was over there, and again with his double tongue setting there what was here, and turning all to hate that formerly was love.'

1.289. βέβακα, Doric for βέβηκα, perf. of βαίνω: ' I have finished my journey.'   ἁ, Doric for ἡ.

1.291. προσέπεσον, see προσπίπτω.

1.292. (The 4th foot is an anapaest.)   τὸ σόν, ' your fate '.

1.294. Talthybius speaks to his men.   ἴτε, pl. imperative of εἶμι.   χρεών [ἐστι], equiv. to χρή, it is necessary.

1.295. ὅσον τάχιστα, equiv. to ὡς τάχιστα, ' as quickly as possible '.

1.296. εἰληγμένας, see λαγχάνω.

1.297. ἄγω, subjunctive of purpose, after ὡς.

1.300. ὡς with participle, because.

1.301. αὐτῶν, ἑαυτῶν.

1.302. θανεῖν, see 17, note.   τοὐλεύθερον, τὸ ἐλεύθερον, ' that which is free '.

1.303. ἐν τοῖς τοιούτοις, neuter, ' in such circumstances as these '.

ll.304–305. τὸ τᾶιδε πρόσφορον ἐχθρὸν δ' Ἀχαιοῖς, ' that which is serviceable to these women but against the cause of the Greeks '.

1.306. Hecuba now speaks in iambics; the calmer metre contrasts with the swift lyric metre of Cassandra's frenzied utterance.

1.308. For Cassandra, see Introduction, 3.   Here she thinks that she is at a shrine (τόδ' ἱερόν).   She speaks to attendants whom she sees in imagination.

l.310. Ὑμέναι' ἄναξ, Hymen, the god of marriage.

l.311. γαμέτας, Doric for γαμέτης. Understand [ἐστιν].

l.313. κατ' Ἄργος, in Argos. She foresees her fate as Agamemnon's prize, and his fate at the hands of his jealous wife. By Apollo's gift she prophesies truly, but because of his curse she is not believed. She speaks throughout of her union with Agamemnon as of a regular marriage. γαμουμένα, Doric for γαμουμένη.

l.315. μᾶτερ, Doric for μῆτερ (vocative). ἐπί, with.

l.317. φίλαν, Doric for φίλην. καταστένουσ' ἔχεις, ' you keep lamenting '.

l.321. αὐγάν, αἴγλαν, Doric for αὐγήν, αἴγλην.

l.323. Ἑκάτα, Doric for Ἑκάτη, a goddess of women, sometimes connected with Artemis and the moon.

l.324a. ᾷ, Doric for ᾗ, relative referring to Ἑκάτα. νόμος ἔχει, ' it is customary '. ' Giving light to you, Hecate, to whom it is the custom. . . .'

l.325. πόδα, see πούς.

l.327. ἐπί governs τύχαις: in, at.

l.329a. ἐν δάφναις. The bay is Apollo's tree. Cassandra seems to have a confused image of Apollo and Hymen as one person; cf. 309–309a; she was Apollo's priestess.

l.333. τᾷδε, Doric for τῇδε, hither. ἐμέθεν, see 260, note.

l.334. φιλτάταν, Doric for φιλτάτην.

l.335. βοάσαθ', βοάσατε, Doric for βοήσατε. Ὑμέναιον, wedding-hymn.

l.337. νύμφαν, Doric for νύμφην: ' in honour of the bride ' (as if βοάσαθ' Ὑμέναιον were one word, a transitive verb).

l.338. καλλίπεπλοι. Cassandra sees not refugees in rags but court ladies in their finest robes.

l.340. εὐνᾷ, Doric for εὐνῇ.

l.342. (The 1st foot is an anapaest.) λήψῃ, see λαμβάνω.

l.343. μή . . . αἴρῃ, purpose clause.

l.344. Ἥφαιστε. Hephaestos was the god of fire. μέν is answered not by δέ but by ἀτάρ.

l.344a. τήνδε. Hecuba now speaks in iambics and does not use the Doric form τάνδε. (No further comment will now be made on Doric ᾱ for η.)

l.345. (The 2nd foot is a tribrach.) ἔξω, ' outside, far different from '.

l.347. γάμους γαμεῖσθαι τούσδε, ' to make this marriage ' (' cognate ' accusative, i.e. the object has the same root meaning as the verb).

l.348. (The 1st foot is an anapaest.) παράδος, see παραδίδωμι. ὀρθά, n. pl., adverbial.

l.350. ἐσωφρονήκασ'. The text is corrupt; it means something like ' have brought you to your right mind '. ἐν ταὐτῷ, ἐν τῷ αὐτῷ, ' in the same state '.

l.351. (The 1st foot is a tribrach and the 3rd a dactyl.)

l.352. (The 2nd foot is a tribrach.) μέλεσι, see μέλος.

l.353. Cassandra now speaks in iambics.

l.355. κἄν, καὶ ἐάν. τἀμά, τὰ ἐμά, ' my affairs '; she means ' I '.

l.356. ἔστι (not ἐστί), ' exists, lives '. Λοξίας, Apollo, in his aspect as god of oracles; see 313, note.

l.357. (The 1st foot is an anapaest.) Ἑλένης, gen. of comparison. γάμον, see 347, note. Here there is an ordinary object also (με).

l.358. (The 4th foot is a tribrach.)

l.359. κἀντι-, καὶ ἀντι-

l.360. ποινάς, vengeance.

l.361. (The 3rd foot is a dactyl.) ἄττα, ' some things '; see τις (enclitic). πέλεκυν. She prophesies of the axe, the instrument of her own death and of Agamemnon's.

l.362. (The 3rd foot is a dactyl.) εἶσι. εἶμι is used as the future of ἔρχομαι. Cassandra is prophesying. χἀτέρων, καὶ ἑτέρων.

l.363. μητροκτόνους τ' ἀγῶνας. Seeing still further into the future, she speaks of the slaying of the guilty Clytaemnestra by the queen's own son, Orestes. All this she exultingly attributes to her own ' marriage ' with Agamemnon.

l.364. θήσουσιν, see τίθημι. Ἀτρέως. Atreus was the father of Agamemnon and Menelaus.

l.365. (The 4th foot is a tribrach.) δείξω, see δείκνυμι.

l.366. ἔνθεος, fem. adj. μέν is here answered by ἀλλά.

l.367. τοσόνδε, ' thus much, to this extent '. στήσομαι, see ἵστημι.

l.368. (The 1st foot is a dactyl.) οἵ, relative, referring to the Greeks. μίαν, see εἷς. Κύπριν, Aphrodite (of Cyprus); love.

E

1.369. (The 2nd foot is a tribrach.) ἀπώλεσαν, see ἀπόλλυμι.

1.370. (The 3rd foot is a tribrach.) στρατηγός, Agamemnon. ἐχθίστων (governed by ὕπερ) refers to Helen. (ἔχθιστος, superl. of ἐχθρός.)

1.371. ὤλεσε, see ὄλλυμι. οἴκοθεν qualifies ἡδόνας. Trans.: ' giving up for his brother the pleasure he had in his children at home, and all for the sake of a woman.' The reference to Agamemnon's children reminds us of how he sacrificed his daughter, Iphigeneia, to Artemis, to ensure fair winds for the fleet at the outset of the war, ten years ago.

1.373. καὶ ταῦτα, ' and that too, and at that '. κοὐ, καὶ οὐ. λελησμένης, see ληΐζω.

1.374. ἤλυθον, ἦλθον (the Greeks). Σκαμανδρίους, adj.; see 29, note.

1.375. (The 3rd foot is a dactyl.) ἔθνησκον. The imperfect here indicates repeated action: ' they died in their hundreds.' ἀποστερέω, rob someone of, usually takes gen. of the thing, but sometimes acc., as here (ὅρια, πατρίδα).

1.376. οὓς δ' Ἄρης ἕλοι, ' but those such as Ares took '. Ares was god of war. ἕλοι, 3rd. sing. aor. opt. act. of αἱρέω, εἷλον. (Optative in an Indefinite clause in past time.)

1.377. εἶδον, see ὁράω. χεροῖν, dative dual of χείρ.

1.378. συνεστάλησαν, see συστέλλω.

1.379. τὰ δ' . . . ἐγίγνετο, ' things at home were happening in the same way for them.' ὅμοια is predicative.

1.380. ' Women were dying widowed, and men were dying childless at home.'

1.381. ἄλλοις, ' for others ' (not with δόμοις). ἐκθρέψαντες, see ἐκτρέφω.

1.382. αὐτῶν, with τάφοις. αἷμα, ' a blood-offering ' (made to the dead, not to the earth).

1.384. τὰ σχρά, τὰ αἰσχρά. ἀμείνων, comparative of καλός, ' better '.

1.385. γένοιτο, optative of wish; see γίγνομαι.

1.386. τὸ κάλλιστον κλέος, in apposition to the sentence. κάλλιστος, superl. of καλός.

1.387. ἕλοι, see 376, note.

1.388. (The 3rd foot is a dactyl.)

1.389. (The 3rd foot is a dactyl.) εἶχον, imperfect from ἔχω.

l.390. χερσίν, see χείρ. περισταλέντες, see περιστέλλω.

l.391. ὅσοι δὲ μὴ θάνοιεν, ' but all those who did not die ';
Indefinite Clause; see 376, note. θάνοιεν, see 17, note.

l.392. κατ᾽ ἦμαρ, ' day by day '.

l.393. ᾤκουν, see οἰκέω. Ἀχαιοῖς . . . ἡδοναί, ' for the Greeks
there was no pleasure in these '. ἀπῆσαν, see ἄπειμι.

l.444. Cassandra now changes from iambics to a trochaic line
of 15 syllables; see Introduction, 8. ἐξακοντίζω, hurl forth,
ejaculate, proclaim loudly. (Ὀδυσσέως, see 273, note.)

l.445. To Talthybius. ὅπως τάχιστα, as ὡς τάχιστα. ἐς ᾽Αιδου
νυμφίῳ γημώμεθα, ' may I marry into the house of Hades, marry
the bridegroom.' (γημώμεθα, aor. subj. mid. of γαμέω: note pl. for
sing., common in Tragedy.)   Prophetic, as she sees her future
union with Agamemnon as causing his death and hers.

l.446. To Agamemnon. ταφήσῃ, see θάπτω. νυκτός, see νύξ.

l.447. (The 5th foot is a tribrach.) Δαναϊδῶν, patronymic; see
230, note and 461, note.

l.448. κἀμέ, καὶ ἐμέ. ἐκβεβλημένην, see ἐκβάλλω.

l.449. (The 1st foot is a tribrach.) ὕδατι, see ὕδωρ.

l.450. δώσουσιν, see 80, note. δάσασθαι (see δατέομαι, divide),
infin. of purpose after δώσουσιν.

l.451. (θεῶν is one syllable and εὔια is three.)

l.452. ἐκλέλοιπα, see ἐκλείπω.

l.453. (The 1st foot is a tribrach.) χρωτός (see χρώς), gen.
with ἀπό. οὖσα, see εἰμί. χρόα (see χρώς), acc. of respect.

l.454. αὔραις, dat. of instrument. σοι, dat. with δῶ (see δίδωμι).
φέρεσθαι, see 450, note.

l.455. ποῦ [ἐστι]. ποτε (unaccented) is often added to a
question; cf. our idiom in ' Whoever is that? ', ' Wherever is
it? '

l.456. οὐκέτ᾽ ἂν φθάνοις ἂν καραδοκῶν, an urgent command,
addressed to Talthybius: ' You could not now be too quick in
watching for. . . .' (One ἄν would be sufficient for the sense.)

l.457. τριῶν, see τρεῖς. Ἐρινύν. The three Ἐρινύες were the
Avenging Furies. χθονός, see χθών.

l.458. δακρύσῃς μηδέν. μή with an aorist subjunctive expresses
prohibition.

l.459. χώ, καὶ ὁ. τεκών, see τίκτω.

l.460. οὐ μακράν, ' in no long time '. δέξεσθε, see δέχομαι.

l.461. πέρσασα, see 72, note. 'Ατρειδῶν, see 364, note. The suffix -ίδης means ' son of, descendant of '. ἀπωλόμεσθα, see ἀπόλλυμι. ὧν . . . ὕπο, ὑφ' ὧν, ' at whose hands '.

l.505. ὕπο, because of.

l.506. (The 1st foot is a tribrach.)

l.507. (The 3rd foot is a tribrach.)

l.508. (The 1st foot is a tribrach.) ἀποφθαρῶ, aor. subj. pass. of ἀποφθείρω.

l.509. (The 1st foot is an anapaest.) καταξανθεῖσα, aor. part. pass. of καταξαίνω, tear in pieces, waste away.

l.510. μηδένα, not οὐδένα, because νομίζετε is imperative. πρὶν ἂν θάνῃ, ' before (until) he dies '.

l.511. The Chorus chants in lyric metre. (Some Doric forms occur here.) στρ. and ἀντ. in the margin stand for *strophe* and *antistrophe*, one section answering the other. The ode begins with the formula of a hymn. A free paraphrase is given in the Appendix. ἀμφί with acc., concerning.

l.513. ἄεισον, aor. imperative of ἀείδω (ᾄδω).

l.516. τετραβάμονος, cf. τριτοβάμονος, 275.   The four-footed chariot is the horse on wheels.

l.517. ὀλόμαν (see ὄλλυμι), ' I was destroyed '. δοριάλωτος, m. and f., ' taken in war '.

l.519. ἔλιπον, see 1, note. οὐράνια, n.pl., internal acc., object of βρέμοντα: ' terribly ' or ' with sounds that reached to heaven '.

l.520. ἔνοπλον, ' with arms inside it '.

l.522. ἀνά, adv., often written as a prefix to a verb; see ἀναβοάω.

l.523. σταθείς, see ἵστημι. ἀπο πέτρας σταθείς, ' from the rock where they stood '.

l.524. The words of the people, quoted by the Chorus. πεπαυμένοι, see παύω.

l.526. The Zeus-born maiden is Athena.

l.527. ἔβα, see βαίνω.

l.528. οὐ, with [ἔβα], not with γεραιός.

l.529. κεχαρμένοι, perf. part. mid. of χαίρω, make glad.

l.530. ἔσχον (see ἔχω), ' gained possession of '.

l.532. ὡρμάθη, see ὁρμάω.

l.535. θέᾳ, ' for a spectacle '; not from θεά, goddess. δώσων (see 80, note), masc., as if λαός had been used instead of γέννα.

l.536. χάριν, ' as a gift of honour '. ἀμβροτοπώλου, adj., ' of the immortal horses '; one of the titles of Athena is Ἱππία.

l.537. ναός, poetic gen. of ναῦς.

l.539. ἕδρανα, pl. for sing., ' dwelling-place '.

l.541. θέσαν, see τίθημι, Epic for ἔθεσαν.

l.542. Take ἐπεί first.

l.544. Not part of the 'when' clause. ἐκτύπει imperfect of κτυπέω.

l.545. μέλεα, contracted in Attic to μέλη.

l.546. ἀέριον, ' lifted high '; it refers grammatically to κρότον, but in sense to the feet. ἀνά, ' all the time with '.

l.550. ἄκος, ' as a remedy '. ἔδωκεν, see 253, note. ὕπνῳ, indirect object.

l.551. ὀρεστέραν . . . παρθένον Διὸς κόραν, Artemis, sister of Apollo and goddess of the forests; also of the moon (see 323, note).

l.556. πτόλιν, πόλιν. κατεῖχε (see κατέχω), ' filled, possessed '. Περγάμων. Pergama was the citadel of Troy.

l.558. ἔβαλλε, sing. with n.pl. subject.

l.559. ἐπτοημένας, perf. part. pass. of πτοέω, terrify.

l.560. ἐξέβαινε, see ἐκβαίνω: note tense. Ἄρης, god of war.

l.561. ἔργα refers to the events, not to Ares.

l.564. καράτομος ἐρημία, ' desolation caused by the beheading (of their husbands) '.

l.565. νεανίδων στέφανον . . . κουροτρόφον, ' the crown (glory) of the young women, the honour of bringing up sons . . .' The girls would be carried off to Greece, to bear the sons of Greeks.

l.568. τήνδε, here.

l.569. ὄχοις, pl. for sing.

l.570. παρὰ δ'εἰρεσίᾳ μαστῶν, ' with her as she beats her breast '.

l.572. To Andromache.

l.575. οἷσιν, οἷς. Ἀχιλλέως παῖς, Pyrrhus Neoptolemus. Φθιώτης, adj., ' from Phthia '.

l.576. στέψει, see στέφω. ἀπὸ Τροίας, ' [having taken them] from Troy '.

l.634. ὦ μῆτερ, ὦ τεκοῦσα, ' you, her mother, you who bore her (Polyxena) '; see 459, note.

l.635. ἄκουσον, ὡς ... ' hear how I shall. . . .' ἐμβαλῶ, future of ἐμβάλλω. ὡς, as ὅπως.

l.636. τὸ μὴ γενέσθαι (see γίγνομαι), ' not to have been born '. Note that the infin. is a neuter noun, used with any case of the article.

l.637. ζῆν, infin. of ζάω. κρείσσων, used as comparative of ἀγαθός. κατθανεῖν, καταθανεῖν.

l.638. ᾐσθημένος, perf. part. of αἰσθάνομαι, which takes a genitive. ' The dead man has no pain from feeling his sorrows.'

l.639. πεσών, see πίπτω.

l.640. ψυχήν, acc. of respect, ' in thought '. ἀλάομαι (wander from, miss) governs the genitive.

l.641. κείνη, ἐκείνη. ἰδοῦσα, see ὁράω.

l.642. τέθνηκε, see θνήσκω. κοὐδέν, καὶ οὐδέν. αὐτῆς, ἑαυτῆς.

l.644. λαχοῦσα, see 244a, note. πλείων, comparative of πολύς. τύχης depends on ἡμάρτανον.

l.645. ἔσθ', ἐστί: auxiliary with ηὑρημένα, making perf. pass. of εὑρίσκω; see also 558, note.

l.646. ἐξεμόχθουν, see ἐκμοχθέω. Note tense: ' I tried hard to achieve.' She is not congratulating herself on achievement.

l.647. ἔνθα, where (relative); the sentence is broken off and continued on different lines. κἄν, καὶ ἐάν. προσῇ, subj. of πρόσεστι.

l.648. ἐφέλκεται, middle.

l.649. ἥτις. The sentence is irregular: εἴ τις (fem.) would be grammatical and would give much the same sense. κακῶς ἀκούειν, ' scandal '.

l.650. (The 3rd foot is an anapaest.) τούτου, ' of not staying at home '. παρεῖσα, aor. part. of παρίημι.

l.651. (The 2nd foot is a tribrach.) κομψὰ ἔπη, ' gossip '.

l.652. εἰσεφρούμην, see εἰσφρέω, let in.

l.653. (The 1st foot is a dactyl.) ἔχουσα ... ἐξήρκουν ἐμοί, ' I contented myself with having '.

l.655. παρεῖχον, see παρέχω. ᾔδη, see οἶδα. ἀμέ, ἃ ἐμέ. ἃ is acc. respect: ' in what things '.

l.656. κείνῳ, see 641, note. παριέναι, see παρίημι, yield, allow.
And I knew in what things I ought to have the victory over my husband, and in what I ought to yield the victory to him.'

l.707. δέδορκα, perf. of δέρκομαι, with present meaning, ' I see '. τόνδε, see 568, note.

l.709. ἄριστος, superl. of ἀγαθός. πρίν ποτε, with Ἕκτορος, not with δάμαρ.

l.711. Δαναῶν, see 230, note. Πελοπιδῶν, the descendants of Pelops, i.e. Agamemnon and Menelaus. Pelops was the father of Atreus.

l.712. φροίμιον, contracted from προοίμιον.

l.713. ἔδοξε, ' it has seemed (good) ', ' it has been decided '. Cf. Latin ' visum est '. εἴπω, aor. subj. of λέγω, subj. of deliberative question.

l.714. μῶν, equiv. to ἆρα μή. ' Surely they have not decided that he is not to have the same master as I? '

l.716. αὐτοῦ, ' just here '; it emphasizes ἐνθάδε. λιπεῖν depends on ἔδοξε.

l.718. ἐπήνεσα, see ἐπαινέω.

l.719. κτενοῦσι, see κτείνω. πύθῃ, aor. subj. of πυνθάνομαι.

l.720. γάμων. She means a forced union with an enemy. ὡς, exclamatory, ' how! ' μείζων, comparative of μέγας.

l.721. Ὀδυσσεύς, see 277, note. Πανέλλησιν, πᾶσι τοῖς Ἕλλησιν.

l.722. (The 3rd foot is a dactyl.) οὐ μέτρια, ' not moderate ', i.e. ' excessive '; a typically Greek expression.

l.723. μὴ τρέφειν, indirect command. (This is rarely found after λέγω.)

l.724. τοιαῦτα νικήσειε, optative of wish : ' May such decisions prevail! ' τῶν, masc. αὐτοῦ, ἑαυτοῦ.

l.725. ῥῦψαι . . . δεῖν σφε (ἔδοξε), ' they have decided that they (σφε) must hurl him '. ῥῦψαι, see ῥίπτω.

l.726. ὡς, equiv. to οὕτως. γενέσθω, 3rd sing. aor. imperative of γίγνομαι. σοφωτέρα (note accent), fem. sing. nom. φανῇ, see φαίνομαι.

l.727. τοῦδε, masc. ἄλγει, 2nd sing. pres. imper. act.

l.728. μηδέν, with σθένουσα. (The second negative does not here cancel the first.) δόκει, as ἄλγει.

l.732. οἷοί τε [ἐσμεν], ' we are able '. οὐ, with βούλομαι in 734. ἐρᾶν. The subject of the infin. is σε. See 733.

l.736. οὔτ' ἂν ταφείη, ' he would not be buried '. ταφείη, aor. opt. pass. of θάπτω. τύχοι, aor. opt. act. of τυγχάνω.

l.737. κεκτημένη, perf. part. mid. of κτάομαι, get, receive.

l.738. οὐκ ἂν λίποις (optative), ' you would not leave '.

l.738. ἄθαπτον. Not to be buried after death was in the eyes of the ancients the utmost outrage a man could suffer. Compare the theme of the Antigone of Sophocles and the errand of Priam to Achilles in the last book of the Iliad; also the fate of Priam as described by Vergil in Aeneid II.

l.739. αὐτή, ' you yourself '. πρευμενέστερος, compar. of πρευμενής, gentle.

l.740. φίλτατε, τιμηθείς, both masc., according to the sense, not neuter to agree with τέκνον. περισσά, n.pl. adj. used as adv.

l.742. δέ, equiv. to καί at the beginning of the line.

l.744. τὸ ἐσθλόν, adj. as noun, ' courage '. ἐς καιρόν, ' at the right time '.

l.745. τἀμά, τὰ ἐμά. Take τε after λέκτρα.

l.747. (The 1st foot is a dactyl.) σφάγιον, predicative, ' as a victim '. τέξουσα, see τίκτω.

l.748. (The 3rd foot is a tribrach.) τύραννον, king or ruler, not tyrant.

l.749. σέθεν, equiv. to σου.

l.750. δέδραξαι, from δράσσομαι (perf. δέδραγμαι), lay hold of (with gen.). χεροί, see χείρ. κἀντέχῃ, καὶ ἀντέχῃ.

l.751. (The 3rd foot is a dactyl.) εἰσπίτνων, equiv. to εἰσπίπτων.

l.752. εἶσιν, from εἶμι, used as future of ἔρχομαι: ' he will come '.

l.753. γῆς, ' from the earth '.

l.754. Understand εἶσιν.

l.755. ἐς τράχηλον . . . πεσών, ' breaking your neck '; see 639, note.

l.756. ἀπορρήξεις, see ἀπορρήγνυμι.

l.757. (The 1st foot is a dactyl.)

l.758. διὰ κενῆς ἄρα, ' in vain then '.

l.759. ἐξέθρεψε, see ἐκτρέφω.

l.760. κατεξάνθην, see καταξαίνω.

l.761. οὔποτ' αὖθις, a statement (not a command, which would have μήποτ'): ' you will never do it again '.

l.762. πρόσπιτνε, as πρόσπιπτε. ἀμφί, with ἕλισσε: ' Twine your arms round my shoulders.'

1.763. ἄρμοσον, ' join (to mine) '.

1.764. ἐξευρόντες, see ἐξευρίσκω.   βάρβαρος is the opposite of
Ἕλλην, ' un-Greek '.

1.765. οὐδέν, acc. of respect, ' in nothing '.

1.766. Τυνδάρειον ἔρνος, offspring of Tyndareos.   T. was the
husband of Leda, whose children were said to be the offspring
of Zeus. Andromache refers here to Helen. Διός, gen. of Ζεύς.

1.767. (The 2nd foot is a tribrach.)   ἐκπεφυκέναι, perf. infin.
act. (with passive meaning) of ἐκφύω, beget.

1.770. Ζῆνα, equiv. to Δία; see 17, note.

1.772. ὄλοιο, aor. opt. mid. of ὄλλυμι: opt. of wish.

1.773. (The 3rd foot is a tribrach.)

1.774. (The 1st foot is a dactyl, the 2nd a tribrach; the two
resolved feet give speed to the line.)   ἄγετε, ' come now '. δοκεῖ,
impersonal, ' it seems good (to you)'.

1.776. οὐ δυναίμεθ᾽ ἄν, ' we would not be able '.

1.777. (The 1st foot is a tribrach.)   δέμας. She means her
own.

1.778. (The 3rd foot is a dactyl.)   ναῦς, acc. pl.

1.779. (The 1st foot is an anapaest, the 2nd a tribrach.)
ὑμέναιον. Andromache, like Cassandra, is thinking of her coming
union with a nenemy. ἀπολέσασα; see 369, note.

1.781. μιᾶς γυναικός, Helen. λέχους, gen. sing. χάριν, following
a gen., because of.

1.782. Talthybius speaks in a lyric metre. ἄγε, see 774, note.
μεθείς, see μεθίημι.

1.784. στεφάνας, crowns, i.e. battlements.

1.785. ἐκράνθη, see κραίνω, accomplish, ordain.

1.787 ὅστις. Understand the antecedent ἐκεῖνον.

1.789. γνώμης, gen. of comparison. μᾶλλον, compar. of μάλα.
' And is more friendly to shamelessness than my mind is.'

1.860. Menelaus has entered while the Chorus sings.

1.862. (The 1st foot is an anapaest.)

1.863. (The 1st foot is an anapaest.)   καὶ στράτευμ᾽ Ἀχαϊκόν,
' and with me the Greek host [ἐμόχθησεν] '.

1.864. Τροίαν, ' to Troy '. οὐχ ὅσον δοκοῦσί με, ' not so much as
men think I did '.

l.866. (The 3rd foot is a dactyl.) ἐλήσατο, see ληίζομαι.

l.867. δίκην διδόναι, ' to be punished '. δέδωκε, sing. verb; the subject is αὐτός, with γῆ added as an afterthought. σὺν θεοῖς, ' with the help of the gods '.

l.868. (The 3rd foot is a dactyl.)

l.870. (The 1st foot is a tribrach.)

l.872 κατηρίθμηται, see καταριθμέω.

l.874. κτανεῖν, κτανών, strong aor. of κτείνω. (The usual prose form is weak and appears in compounds; e.g. ἀπέκτεινα. ἔδοσαν, see δίδωμι. εἴτε μὴ κτανὼν θέλοιμ' ἄγεσθαι, ' or else, if I wished it, to take her back without having killed her '.

l.875. (The 3rd foot is a dactyl.) θέλοιμι, pres. opt.

l.877. (The 1st foot is an anapaest.) ἐᾶσαι, ' give up '.

l.878. κᾆτα, καὶ εἶτα. κτανεῖν, ' for the slaying '; infin. of purpose with δοῦναι.

l.879. ποινὰς ὅσοις ... φίλοι, ' revenge for all my friends who ...' τεθνᾶσι, contracted from τεθνήκασι: see 642, note.

l.881. τῆς ... κόμης, ' by the hair '.

ll.882–3. ὅταν ... μόλωσι, Indefinite temporal clause with subj. μόλωσι, see βλώσκω.

l.883. Ἑλλάδα, see 864, note.

l.884. κἀπί, καὶ ἐπί.

l.885. δυστόπαστος, nom., not voc., agreeing with σύ, subject of εἶ. εἰδέναι, infin. of οἶδα: ' epexegetic ' or explanatory infin., explaining δυστόπαστος.

l.886. (The 3rd foot is a dactyl.) Ζεύς, nom.; see 885, note. φύσεος, φύσεως.

l.887. προσηυξάμην, see προσεύχομαι. πάντα, with τὰ θνητά.

l.889. ὡς, exclamatory. ' New prayers indeed have you made to the gods! '

l.890. (The 2nd foot is a tribrach.)

l.891. ὁρᾶν, object of φεῦγε. ' Flee from the sight of her.' ἕλῃ (see αἱρέω), subjunctive in purpose clause. The Greeks liked a play on words, and ἕλῃ recalls Ἑλένη.

ll.892–3. Compare Marlowe, *Doctor Faustus*, 1336–7:

' Was this the face that launched a thousand ships
    And burnt the topless towers of Ilium? '

l.894. χοί, καὶ οἱ. πεπονθότες, see πάσχω.

l.895. (The 1st foot is an anapaest.) φροίμιον, see προοίμιον.

l.896. σέθεν, σοῦ.

l.898. σχεδόν . . . οἶδά σοι μισουμένη, ' I know, well-nigh for certain, that I am hated by you '. Note the participle, not infin., with οἶδα: it is nom., not acc., as it refers to the subject of οἶδα.

l.899. ἐρέσθαι, see ἐρωτάω. γνῶμαι τίνες [εἰσὶν] Ἕλλησι καὶ σοί; ' What intentions have you and the Greeks? '

l.901. οὐκ εἰς ἀκριβὲς ἦλθες, ' your case did not come to a formal discussion '.

l.902. κτανεῖν . . . ἔδωκεν, see 878, note. ἠδίκεις, see ἀδικέω.

l.904. ἤν, ἐάν. θάνω, aor. subj. of θνῄσκω. θανούμεθα, pl. for sing.

l.905. ἐλήλυθα, see ἔρχομαι.

l.906. τοῦδε ἐνδεής, ' without a hearing '.

l.907. (The 1st foot is an anapaest.) δός, see δίδωμι.

l.908. ἡμῖν, pl. for sing.

l.909. κάτοισθα, see κάτοιδα, understand. συντιθείς, pres. part. act. of συντίθημι.

l.910. ὥστε . . . φυγεῖν, expresses result; see φεύγω.

l.911. σχολῆς τὸ δῶρον, ' to grant the boon needs leisure '.

l.912. μάθῃ, see 63, note.

l.913. τῆσδε . . . χάριν, ' the favour which she asks '.

l.914. κἄν, καὶ ἐάν.

l.915. (The 3rd foot is a dactyl.)

ll.916–18. ' But as regards the charges which I think, if you argue (go through reasons), you will bring against me, I will answer, setting my accusations against yours and yours [against mine].'

l.916. ἰόντα, see εἶμι.

l.917. ἀντιθεῖσα, see ἀντιτίθημι.

l.918. τἀμά, τὰ ἐμά.

l.919. ἔτεκεν, see 459, note. ἥδε. Helen indicates Hecuba.

l.921. κἄμ', καὶ ἐμέ. ὁ πρέσβυς, Priam.

l.922. δαλοῦ πικρὸν μίμημα, ' baleful semblance of a fire-brand '. See Introduction, 3. Ἀλέξανδρος was the other name of Paris; it means ' defending men ', and may be the Greek translation of the Phrygian name Paris.

l.923. τἀπίλοιπ', τὰ ἐπίλοιπα. ὡς ἔχει, ' how they stand '.

l.924. ζεῦγος, usually a yoke of oxen or a pair of anything; cf. ζεύγνυμι, join. ὅδε, Paris. τριῶν θεῶν, fem.; see Introduction, 3.

l.925. δόσις, ' the offered gift '.

l.927. ὑπέσχετο, see ὑπισχνέομαι.

l.928. τυραννίδ' ἕξειν, ' that he should have as his absolute kingdom '. ἕξειν, see ἔχω. εἴ σφε κρίνειεν (aor. opt.), ' if he should prefer her '.

l.929. Κύπρις, see 368, note. τοὐμόν, τὸ ἐμόν.

l.930. ὑπερδράμοι, aor. opt. from ὑπερτρέχω, outrun, excel.

l.931. τὸν ἐνθένδε . . . λόγον, ' the rest of the tale '. ὡς ἔχει, see 923, note. σκέψαι, aor. imperative of σκέπτομαι.

l.932. (θεάς, one syllable here.) τοσόνδε, ' to this extent '. οὑμοί, οἱ ἐμοί.

l.933. ὤνησαν, see ὀνίνημι. ἐκ, as ὑπό.

l.934. Trans: ' Neither having faced the spears in battle nor having submitted to a tyranny.' σταθέντες, see 523, note.

l.935. ἅ, ' in respect to the things in which '.

l.936. πραθεῖσα, see πέρνημι. κὠνειδίζομαι, καὶ ὀνειδίζομαι.

l.937. (The 3rd and 4th feet are tribrachs.) ἐξ ὧν, ' by those at whose hands '. λαβεῖν, see 26, note.

l.938. αὐτὰ τὰν ποσίν, ' the very matters close at hand '. τὰν, τὰ ἐν. ποσίν, see πούς.

l.939. ἀφώρμησα, see ἀφορμάω.

l.940. (The 3rd foot is a dactyl.) ἦλθ', 3rd person.

l.941. τῆσδε, ' my own '.

l.942. νιν, αὐτόν.

l.944. Σπάρτης, from Sparta. ἀπῆρας, see ἀπαίρω. νηί, see ναῦς. Κρησίαν χθόνα, ' to the Cretan land '. Sparta is inland, on the river Eurotas, which can scarcely have been navigable at any time; in her excitement, Helen leaves out a stage in her account of the journey: ' From Sparta you [went and] set out by ship for the land of Crete.'

l.945. (σέ, ἀλλ'. Run together, as one syllable.) τοὐπὶ (τὸ ἐπὶ) τῷδε, ' what happened after this '. ἐρήσομαι, see ἐρωτάω.

l.946. ἑσπόμην, see ἕπομαι.

l.947. (The 3rd foot is a tribrach.) προδοῦσα, see προδίδωμι.

1.948. θεόν (one syllable here), Aphrodite. γενοῦ, aor. imperative of γίγνομαι.

1.950. The many love-affairs of Zeus are notorious. συγγνώμη δ' [ἔστιν] ἐμοί, ' but I am excused '.

1.961. θνήσκοιμ' ἄν, 'I should die'; optative. A repeated ἄν is not uncommon. πρὸς σοῦ, ' in your eyes '.

1.963. τὰ δ' οἴκοθεν κεῖν', ' but as to my life in his house '.

1.965. τὸ χρῄζειν . . . σου τόδε, ' this desire of yours '.

1.966. (The 1st foot is an anapaest.)

1.967. πειθώ, acc. sing.

1.969. θεαῖσι (two syllables), Hera and Athena, who were hostile to Paris because he slighted them; see Introduction, 3. πρῶτα, n.pl., adverbial.

1.970. δείξω, see 365, note. Trans: ' And if she is not saying what is right, I will show that she isn't.'

1.972. (The 3rd foot is a tribrach.) οὐκ ἐς τοσοῦτον . . . ἐλθεῖν, ' have not reached such a pitch '.

1.973. ἥ (demonstrative), Hera. ἀπημπόλα, see ἀπεμπολάω: note tense, ' was for betraying '.

1.974. Παλλάς, understand ἀπημπόλα. δουλεύειν, infin. of purpose, after δίδωμι.

1.975. παιδιαῖσι καὶ χλιδῇ, ' in mere sport and wantonness '.

1.976. Ἴδην, see Introduction, 3. τοῦ, interrog. ἄν . . . ἔσχε, ' would she have had '.

1.978. (The 1st foot is a tribrach.) Trans: ' Was it so that she might get . . .? ' ἀμείνων, compar. of ἀγαθός.

1.979. (The 1st foot is a dactyl; θεῶν is one syllable.) θηρωμένη, middle.

1.981. (The 4th foot is an anapaest.) ποίει, imperative (note accent). μή with pres. imper. means ' stop doing! '

1.982. κακόν, ' wickedness '. μὴ οὐ πείσῃς, ' lest you fail to persuade '; see πείθω.

1.984. (The 4th foot is a tribrach.) Μενέλεω, genitive.

1.985. οὐκ ἄν . . . ' could she not have . . .? ' ἥσυχος, fem.

1.986. αὐταῖς Ἀμύκλαις, ' Amyclae and all '. A. was a town near Sparta. ἤγαγεν, see ἄγω.

1.987. οὑμός, ὁ ἐμός. κάλλος, acc. of respect.

l.988. 'And your heart, having beheld him, was transformed into Aphrodite.'

l.989. (The 4th foot is a tribrach.)

l.990. (The 3rd foot is a dactyl.) τοὔνομ', τὸ ὄνομα. ἀφροσύνης ἄρχει, ' has in it the beginning of the word ἀφροσύνη '.

l.992. ἐξεμαργώθης, see ἐκμαργόομαι. φρένας, acc. of respect.

l.994. ἀπαλλαχθεῖσα, see 270, note.

l.996. (The 1st foot is an anapaest, the 3rd a dactyl and the 5th a tribrach.)

l.998. ἄγειν, pres. infin. representing imperf. indic.

l.999. Σπαρτιατῶν, 'of the Spartan citizens'. ᾔσθετο, see αἰσθάνομαι.

l.1001. ὄντος, participle in gen. abs., ' existing ', i.e. ' on earth '. Κάστορος . . . πω, ' while C., yet a young man, still lived, and his brother also, and neither was yet among the stars '. Castor and Polydeuces (Pollux) were the twin brothers of Helen. The story said (as so often with twins) that one was immortal and the other not. Polydeuces was allowed to share his immortality with Castor, so that when C. died they took it in turns to be ' among the stars '.

l.1020. ὕβριζες, imperfect (ῡ).

l.1022. (The 1st foot is a tribrach.) κἀπὶ (καὶ ἐπὶ) τοῖσδε, ' and after all this '.

l.1023. κἄβλεψας, καὶ ἔβλεψας. πόσει τὸν αὐτὸν αἰθέρ', ' the same sky as your husband '.

l.1026. κρᾶτα, acc. of respect. ἀπεσκυθισμένην, perf. part. pass. of ἀποσκυθίζω, shave bare or scalp (derived from Σκύθης, because of the barbarous habits of the Scythians).

ll.1027–8. τὸ σῶφρον . . . ἡμαρτημένοις, ' if you had more proper feeling than shamelessness towards your errors '. ἡμαρτημένοις, perf. part. pass. of ἁμαρτάνω.

l.1028. (The 2nd foot is a tribrach.)

l.1029. (The 1st foot is an anapaest.) εἰδῇς, see 86, note. οἷ, ' whither, how '.

l.1030. (The 1st foot is an anapaest.)

l.1031. σαυτοῦ, gen. with ἀξίως. θές, see τίθημι.

l.1032. θνῄσκειν, infin. of indirect command. ἥτις ἂν προδῷ, ' whoever betrays '; see 947, note.

l.1033. (The 1st foot is an anapaest and the 2nd a tribrach.)

l.1034. τεῖσαι, aor. imperative mid. of τείνω. κἀφελοῦ, καὶ ἀφελοῦ, aor. imper. mid. of ἀφαιρέω. πρός, ' in the eyes of '.

l.1035. ψόγον τὸ θῆλύ τε, ' the reproach and the womanishness ', i.e. ' the reproach of womanishness '; hendiadys. φανείς, see 726, note.

l.1036. ἐμοί, see 1023, note. συμπέπτωκας, see συμπίπτω. ἐς ταὐτὸν (τὸ αὐτὸν) λόγον, ' to the same conclusion '.

l.1037. τήνδε...ἐλθεῖν, acc. with infin., 'namely, that she came'.

l.1038. χἠ, καὶ ἡ.

l.1039. ἐνεῖται, perf. pass. from ἐνίημι, ' has been brought in [to the argument] '. βαῖνε, addressed to Helen.

l.1040. ἀπόδος, see ἀποδίδωμι, atone for. ἐν μικρῷ, ' soon '.

l.1041. οἶδα with (μή and) infin., know how (not) to.

l.1042. (The 2nd foot is a tribrach.) πρός σε γονάτων, ' by your knees [I beseech] you '.

l.1043. προσθείς, see προστίθημι, impute to. συγγίγνωσκε: note tense, ' be forgiving '.

l.1044. ἀπέκτεινε, see ἀποκτείνω. μὴ προδῷς, prohibition; see προδίδωμι.

l.1046. παῦσαι, as τεῖσαι, 1034.

l.1047. λέγω here introduces an indirect command.

l.1049. νεώς, gen. of ναῦς. σοὶ ταὐτόν, see 1036, note. ἐσβήτω, aor. imper. of ἐσβαίνω.

l.1052. ὅπως, ' that is as '. ἐκβῇ, see ἐκβαίνω, turn out.

l.1053. ἐσβήσεται, see ἐσβαίνω.

l.1055. Ἄργος, ' to Argos '. ὥσπερ ἀξία [ἐστίν], ' as she deserves '.

l.1057. θήσει, see 364, note.

l.1059. τὸ μῶρον, ' folly '. κἄν, καὶ ἐάν. ὦσι, subj. of εἰμί (after ἐάν). ἐχθίων, compar. of ἐχθρός.

l.1123. λελειμμένος, see λείπω.

l.1124. τἀπίλοιπα, τὰ ἐπίλοιπα. Ἀχιλλείου τόκου, see 273, note.

l.1125. Φθιώτιδας, see 243, note.

l.1126. (The 4th foot is an anapaest. Νεοπ- is one syllable). ἀνῆκται, see ἀνάγω.

l.1127. (Πηλέως is two syllables.) Peleus was the fat' 1er Achilles. νιν, αὐτόν, meaning Peleus.

l.1128. Acastus, son of Pĕlias, was enemy to Pēleus because he loved Peleus' wife. ἐκβέβληκεν, see ἐκβάλλω.

l.1129. οὖ, neuter. θᾶσσον, compar. of ταχέως. μονῆς, see μονή, and note accent. Trans: 'Being moved by this circumstance rather than because he had any pleasure in staying. . . .'

l.1130. (The 4th foot is an anapaest.)

l.1131. (The 1st foot is an anapaest.) ἀγωγός, fem.: 'she drew from me'. ἐξώρμα, see ἐξορμάω: note tense, 'she was on the point of setting forth'.

l.1133. σφε, him, Neoptolemus.

l.1134. θάψαι [τινά], 'that someone might bury'. νεκρὸν τόνδε. Talthybius indicates the shield, which holds the body of Astyanax.

l.1135. ἀφῆκεν, see ἀφίημι.

l.1136. ἀσπίδα. The shield covered a man's body from neck to feet, and was semi-cylindrical in shape, so that it protected his sides (πλευρά). See L. Cottrell, The Bull of Minos, Great Pan edition, p. 28.

l.1137. ἐβάλλετο: note tense, 'he used to put'. (βάλλω often means 'put', especially in Homer; cf. Mod. Gk. βάζω, ἔβαλα.)

l.1138. (Πηλέως is here 3 syllables.) πορεῦσαι depends on ᾐτήσατο, 1133.

l.1140. λύπας, in apposition to ἀσπίδα. ὁρᾶν, explanatory infin.: 'this shield, a grief for her to see'.

l.1141. (The 3rd foot is a dactyl.)

l.1142. θάψαι, as πορεῦσαι, 1138.

l.1143. περιστείλῃς, see περιστέλλω.

l.1144. (The 1st foot is an anapaest and the 3rd a dactyl.) ὡς ἔχει τὰ σά, 'according to your present circumstances'.

l.1145. βέβηκε, see 289, note.

l.1146. ἀφείλετο, see ἀφαιρέω. αὐτήν, herself. μή, usual after verbs meaning 'prevent' (except κωλύω); not to be translated by a negative.

l.1148. ἐπαμπισχόντες, aor. part. of ἐπαμπέχω. ἀροῦμεν, see αἴρω. δόρυ, here 'mast'.

l.1149. τἀπεσταλμένα, τὰ ἐπε-, see ἐπιστέλλω.

l.1150. ἀπαλλάξας, aor. part. of ἀπαλλάσσω, used here with ἔχω to make a compound tense, 'I have released you'; cf. the use of auxiliary ' have ', etc., in modern English, French and Greek.

l.1151. (The 4th foot is a tribrach.) Σκαμανδρίους . . . ῥοάς, see 29, note.

l.1152. (νεκ-ρόν is here two long syllables, but in 1140 νε-κροῦ is an iambus.) κἀπένιψα, καὶ ἀπένιψα, see ἀπονίζω.

l.1153. εἶμι, as future of ἔρχομαι. ἀναρρήξων, see ἀναρρήγνυμι.

l.1154. τἀπ' ἐμοῦ τε κἀπὸ σοῦ (τὰ ἀπὸ ἐμοῦ τε καὶ ἀπὸ σοῦ), ' my works and yours '.

l.1156. θέσθε, see τίθημι. ἀμφίτορνον, see 1136, note.

l.1157. κοὐ, καὶ οὐ. λεύσσειν, explanatory infin.

l.1158. (The 3rd foot is a dactyl.) Trans: ' O you whose might in war is weightier than your wisdom. . . .' φρενῶν, see φρήν.

l.1159. δείσαντες, see δείδω.

l.1160. διειργάσασθαι, see διεργάζομαι. μή . . . ὀρθώσειεν (optative), ' were you afraid that he might set upright . . .? '

l.1161. οὐδὲν ἦτε, ' you were indeed mere nothings '.

l.1162. Ἕκτορος . . . εὐτυχοῦντος, gen. abs., continued in μυρίας τ'ἄλλης χερός. ἐς δόρυ, ' in battle '.

l.1164. (πόλεως, one syllable.) ἁλούσης, see ἁλίσκομαι. ἐφθαρμένων, see φθείρω.

l.1166. ὅστις, translate: ' when a man '. διεξελθών, see διεξέρχομαι.

l.1167. (The 3rd foot is a dactyl.) ὡς, exclamatory.

l.1168. (The 2nd foot is a tribrach, the 3rd a dactyl.) τυχών, see τυγχάνω.

l.1169. (The 3rd foot is a dactyl.)

l.1170. (The 1st and 5th feet are tribrachs.) ἦσθ'ἄν, ' you would have been '.

l.1171. αὔτ', αὐτά, ' all these things '. ἰδών, see ὁράω. γνούς, see γιγνώσκω. σῇ ψυχῇ, with γνούς.

l.1172. οὐκ οἶσθα, ' you know them not by experience '. οἶδα is here contrasted with γιγνώσκω, know with the mind (ψυχῇ). ἐχρήσω, see χράομαι. οὐδέν, adverbial, with ἐχρήσω.

l.1173. κρατός (see κράς), gen. depending on βόστρυχον, 1175. ὡς, exclamatory. ἔκειρεν governs two objects, σε and βόστρυχον, 1175.

F

l.1174. τείχη, subject of ἔκειρεν. Λοξίου. Loxias is Apollo, who with Poseidon built the ramparts; see 356, note, and Introduction, 3.

l.1175. πολλά, adverbial, ' often, much'.

l.1177. (ὀστέων is two syllables; the 3rd foot is a dactyl.) ῥαγέντων, see ῥήγνυμι. φόνος, here ' blood '.

l.1178. εἰκούς, acc. pl. of εἰκώ, image.

l.1179. κέκτησθε, see κτάομαι; the perfect means ' possess '.

l.1180. πολλά, see 1175, note. ἐκβαλόν, aor. part. act. of ἐκβάλλω.

l.1181. ὄλωλας, see 9, note. ἐψεύσω, see ψεύδομαι. ὅτ' for ὅτε, when.

l.1182. ηὔδας, imperfect from αὐδάω.

l.1183. (The 1st foot is an anapaest.) κεροῦμαι, see κείρω.

l.1184. (The 3rd foot is a dactyl.) ἀπάξω, see ἀπάγω.

l.1186. (The 1st foot is a dactyl and the 2nd a tribrach. All three syllables of ἄτεκνος are short.) ἄτεκνος. Her children are all dead, or else, like Cassandra, taken from her.

l.1189. γράψειεν ἄν, optative, ' would write '. σε, ' about you '.

l.1191. τοὐπι-, τὸ ἐπι-

l.1192. λαχών, see 244a, note.

l.1193. ταφήσῃ, see 446, note.

l.1200. (The 1st foot is a tribrach.)

l.1201. τῶν παρόντων, neuter, ' the things which are at hand '. ἐς κάλλος, ' for the purpose of adornment '.

l.1202. ὧν, ' from those things which '. λήψῃ, see 342, note.

l.1204. βέβαια (as βεβαίως), with εὖ πράσσειν. τοῖς τρόποις, ' in its behaviour '. αἱ τύχαι, pl. for sing.

l.1206. κοὐδείς, καὶ οὐδείς. αὐτός, ' by his own efforts '.

l.1207. καὶ μήν. The Chorus calls our attention to the entrance of some women. πρόχειρον . . . σκυλευμάτων Φρυγίων, ' such as is ready at hand from the loot of Troy '.

l.1208. (The 1st foot is an anapaest.) ἐξάπτειν, infin. of purpose, depending on φέρουσι.

l.1209. νικήσαντα, ' having excelled '. σε, object of θηρωμένη, 1211.

l.1210. ἥλικας, obj. of νικήσαντα.

l.1213. τῶν σῶν ποτ' ὄντων, ' from the wealth which once was yours '.

l.1214. (The 2nd foot is a tribrach.) ἀφείλετο, see 1146, note. πρὸς δέ, ' and besides '.

l.1215. ἐξαπώλεσεν, see ἐξαπόλλυμι.

l.1217. ἔθιγες, see θιγγάνω.

l.1219. προσθέσθαι, see προστίθημι.

l.1219a. (The 1st foot is an anapaest.) γήμαντα, see γαμέω.

l.1220. (The 1st foot is a tribrach.)

l.1221. καλλίνικε, vocative, agreeing with σύ.

l.1223. στεφανοῦ, pres. imper. pass.

ll.1224–5. μᾶλλον ἄξιον [ἐστι] τιμᾶν. . . .

l.1225. ('Ο-δυσ-σέως is 3 syllables.)

l.1227. δέξεται, see δέχομαι.

l.1232. (The 1st foot is an anapaest and the 3rd a dactyl.) ἕλκη, acc. of respect. τὰ μέν, ' some of your wounds '; answered by τὰ δ', 1234.

l.1233. (The 3rd foot is a tribrach.) τἄργα, τὰ ἔργα.

l.1239. σάς, ' your friends '.

l.1240. οὐκ ἦν ἄρ' ἐν θεοῖσι, ' there was nothing then among the gods '; i.e. ' the gods had nothing then in store for me '. οὑμοί, οἱ ἐμοί.

l.1241. (πόλεων is two syllables.)

l.1243. ἔστρεψε, see στρέφω. τἄνω, τὰ ἄνω.

l.1244. (The 1st foot is an anapaest.) ὄντες, masc., referring to her family or to all the Trojans. οὐκ ἂν ὑμνήθημεν, ' we should not have been sung of '. Note ἂν 3 times in one clause; the repetition does not affect the meaning.

l.1247. νερτέρων στέφη, ' wreaths of those below '; i.e. funeral wreaths.

l.1248. (The 4th foot is a tribrach.) διαφέρειν βραχύ, ' it makes little difference '.

l.1249. τεύξεται, see τυγχάνω.

l.1252. μήτηρ, nom., not voc.: ' unhappy is the mother '.

l.1254. Addressed to Astyanax. μέγα, trans. as adverb. ὡς, because.

l.1257. 'Ιλιάσιν, see 'Ιλιάς.

l.1258. χέρας, obj. of διερέσσοντας.

l.1259a. προσέσεσθαι, see πρόσειμι. μέλλω usually takes future infin.

l.1260. οἳ τέταχθε (see τάσσω), ' you who have been ordered '.

l.1261. (The 1st foot is an anapaest.)

l.1262. ἐνιέναι, see ἐνίημι.

l.1263. ὡς ἄν, equiv. to ἵνα.

l.1265. (The 3rd foot is a dactyl.) αὐτός, ὁ αὐτός.

l.1266. ὀρθίαν agrees with ἠχώ, 1267.

l.1267. δῶσιν, see δίδωμι.

l.1270. ('Οδυσσέως is 4 syllables here.)

l.1271. οἵδε. Odysseus' men appear.

l.1272. οἲ 'γώ, οἲ ἐγώ, ' ah me! '

l.1274. (The 2nd foot is a tribrach, the 3rd a dactyl.)

l.1277. (The 1st foot is a dactyl.) ἀμπνέουσα (for ἀναπνέουσα), pres. participle, corresponding to imperf. indic.

l.1278. (The 3rd foot is a tribrach.) ἀφαιρήσῃ, ' you will be robbed of '.

l.1280. (θεοί is one syllable here.)

l.1281. (The 4th foot is a tribrach.)

l.1282. φέρε, ' come '. δράμωμεν, see τρέχω. ὡς, as ὥστε, with verb in infin.: result.

l.1283. (The 2nd foot is a tribrach.) κατθανεῖν, see καταθνήσκω.

l.1285. (The 1st foot is a dactyl.) ἀλλ' ἄγετε. Addressed to the Greek soldiers.

l.1286. γέρας, ' as a gift of honour '.

APPENDIX

A free-verse translation of the Choral Ode, lines 511–567, from F. Kinchin Smith's translation of the play [Sidgwick and Jackson, 1951]: printed here by courtesy of the publishers.

' Sing me, Muse, the doom of Troy,
A funeral hymn with music new,
Sad music of tears.
It was that accursed horse
Which walked on wheels
That brought our ruin.

They left it at the gates—
Clanging ominously—
With its trappings of gold without,
And its load of arms within.
Loud cried our folk
As they stood on the city's rock
" Come out, our troubles pass,
Drag in the sacred image
To offer to Athena, who has saved us! "
And out they came from their homes
Men young and old,
And with cries of joy hauled in the fatal snare.

To the gates they rushed,
To honour the Virgin Goddess,
And dedicate to her this monster,
But the dedication proved an Argive band
Hidden in the pinewood belly
For Troy's destruction.

They dragged it in with hempen ropes,
Like some new ship to its launching,
And set it before Athena's shrine
On stones so soon to drink our country's blood.

Now over their toil and their joy
Black night came down.
The shrill of the Libyan flute
Was mingled with Trojan songs,
And the patter of dancing feet,
While in homes the blaze of torches
Made flickering shadows on sleeping eyes.

I was singing myself that night
As I danced to Artemis, queen of the hills,
When suddenly through the town there rang
A cry of death in the homes of Troy,
And babies clung to their mother's skirts
In terror, as forth from the horse's womb
The soldiers poured, and Athena laughed.
Then the altars ran with Trojan blood,
And girls in beds alone, their men
Beside them headless—a noble triumph
For Greece to nurture children on,
But for our poor land—tribulation.'

VOCABULARY

The principal parts of verbs are not given in full: only those are included which are needed for reading the text; e.g. στρέφω, ἔστρεψα.

Long vowels are marked, except for those final vowels whose length is determined by grammatical rules.

ABBREVIATIONS

acc.	accusative	*interrog.*	interrogative
adj.	adjective	*intr.*	intransitive
adv.	adverb	*m.*	masculine
aor.	aorist	*mid.*	middle
c.	common	*n.*	neuter
comp.	comparative	*opt.*	optative
conj.	conjunction	*pp.*	perfect participle
contr.	contracted	*p.p.p.*	perfect participle
dat.	dative		passive
f.	feminine	*part.*	participle
fut.	future	*pass.*	passive
gen.	genitive	*perf.*	perfect
imperf.	imperfect	*pl.*	plural
impers.	impersonal	*poss.*	possessive
indecl.	indeclinable	*prep.*	preposition
indef.	indefinite	*pron.*	pronoun
infin.	infinitive	*superl.*	superlative
interj.	interjection	*tr.*	transitive

A

ἁβρ-ός, -ά, -όν, graceful, delicate. (ἁ)

ἀγαθ-ός, -ή, -όν, good, brave.

ἄγαλμ-α, -ατος, τό, glory, ornament, gift.

ἀγάλλομαι, exult, glory.

ἀγγέλλω, *fut.* ἀγγελῶ, *aor. pass.* ἠγγέλθην and ἠγγέλην, announce, report.

ἄγγελμ-α, -ατος, τό, message.

ἄγγελ-ος, -ου, ὁ, messenger.

ἀγν-ός, -ή, -όν, holy, pure, virgin.

ἄγχι, *adv.* (*with gen.*), near.

ἄγω, ἤγαγον, lead, bring, fetch.
  See 774, 782, *note*.

ἀγωγ-ός, -όν, leading, drawing
  forth.

ἀγ-ών, -ῶνος, ὁ, struggle, contest.

ἀδελφ-ός, -οῦ, ὁ, brother.

ἀδικέω, do wrong, injure.

ἀεί, always.

ἀείδω, ἄεισα, sing, sing of.

ἀέρι-ος, -α, -ον, high in the air.

ἄζ-υξ, -υγος, ὁ, ἡ, τό, *adj.*, unwedded.

ἄθαπτ-ος, -ον, unburied.

'Αθηναῖ-ος, -α, -ον, Athenian, of
  Athens.

aΑθήν-η, -ης, ἡ, *and* 'Αθην-ᾶ,-ᾶς,
  ἡ, the goddess Athena.

ἄθλι-ος, -α, -ον *and* ἄθλι-ος, -ον,
  wretched, miserable.

αἰαῖ, *interj. of astonishment or
  grief.*

Αἴγαι-ος, -α, -ον, Aegean.

αἴγλ-η, -ης, ἡ, light.

αἰδ-ώς, -οῦς, ὁ, awe, respect,
  sense of shame.

αἰθέρι-ος, -α, -ον *and* αἰθέρι-ος, -ον,
  high in air, heavenly.

αἰθ-ήρ, -έρος, ὁ *and* ἡ, upper air,
  heaven.

αἴθω, cause to burn *or* blaze.

αἷμ-α, -ατος, τό, blood.

αἰνέω, praise, commend.

αἱρέω, εἷλον, take, capture.

αἴρω, *fut.* ἀρῶ, raise, set out.

αἰσθάνομαι, ᾐσθόμην, ᾔσθημαι,
  with gen., perceive, feel.

αἰσχρ-ός, -ά, -όν *and* αἰσχρ-ός, -όν,
  shameful, base.

αἰτέω, ask, beg.

αἰτί-α, -ας, ἡ, guilt, cause.

αἰτίαμ-α, -ατος, τό, charge, accu-
  sation.

αἴτι-ος, -α, -ον, responsible,
  guilty.

αἰχμαλωτικ-ός, -ή, -όν, of a
  prisoner.

αἰχμαλωτ-ίς, -ίδος, ἡ, captive.

αἰχμάλωτ-ος, -ον, taken in war.

αἰχμ-ή, -ῆς, ἡ, spear-point, spear.

ἄκληρ-ος, -ον, having no lot, not
  allotted. See 32, *note*.

ἄκ-ος, -ους, τό, remedy.

ἀκούω, hear; 906, *with gen.*

ἀκρῑβ-ής, -ές, exact, precise.
  See 901, *note*.

ἄκρ-ος, -α, -ον, highest.

ἀκτ-ή, -ῆς, ἡ, coast, headland.

ἀλάομαι, wander; *with gen.*,
  wander from, miss.

ἄλαστ-ος, -ον, unforgettable.

'Αλάστ-ωρ, -ορος, ὁ, avenging
  spirit, evil genius.

ἀλγέω, feel pain, grieve.

ἄλεκτρ-ος, -ον, unwedded.

ἁλίσκομαι, *aor.* ἑάλων, be taken,
  be caught.

ἀλκ-ή, -ῆς, ἡ, strength, courage.

ἀλλά, but.

ἄλλ-ος, -η, -ον, other. See 67, *note*.

ἄλλοσε, to another place.

ἄλλοτε, at another time. See 67,
  note.

ἁλμυρ-ός, -ά, -όν, salt, bitter.

ἄλοχ-ος, -ου, ἡ, wife.

ἅλς, ἁλός, ἡ, sea.

ἄλσ-ος, -ους, τό, grove.

ἅμα, at the same time.

ἀμαθ-ής, -ές, ignorant, stupid.

ἀμαθί-α, -ας, ἡ, ignorance, folly.

ἁμαρτάνω, ἥμαρτον, *perf. pass.*
  ἡμάρτημαι, make a mistake,
  go wrong.

ἀμβροτόπωλ-ος, -ον, of the immortal horses.

ἀμείβομαι, reply.

ἀμείν-ων, -ον, better.

ἀμπισχών, see 14, note.

ἀμύν-ω, ἤμῦνα, ward off.

ἀμφ-ελίσσω, wind round.

ἀμφί, prep. with acc., round, about, concerning.

ἀμφί-βολ-ον, -ου, τό, that which is put round.

ἀμφι-βώμι-ος, -ον, round the altars.

ἀμφί-τορν-ος, -ον, well-rounded.

ἄν, particle in certain types of conditional sentence; see 47, note.

ἀνά, prep. with acc., up and down, throughout.

ἀνα-βοάω, cry aloud.

ἀνα-γελάω, laugh aloud.

ἀνάγκ-η, -ης, ἡ, necessity.

ἀν-άγω, ἀνήγαγον, perf. pass. ἀνῆγμαι, lead up, bring back; mid. and pass., set sail.

ἀν-αίδει-α, -ας, ἡ, shamelessness.

ἀν-αιθύσσω, stir up, rouse.

ἀνα-καλέω, invoke repeatedly.

ἀνάκτορ-ον, -ου, τό, palace, temple.

ἀνάκτ-ωρ, -ορος, ὁ, as ἄναξ.

ἄναξ, ἄνακτος, ὁ, lord, master.

ἀναρ-ρήγνῦμι, ἀναρρήξω, break up, dig up.

ἄνασσ-α, -ης, ἡ, lady, queen.

ἀνά-στασ-ις, -εως, ἡ, removal, desolation.

ἀνα-στένω, groan aloud for.

ἀνα-στρέφομαι, dwell.

ἀνα-φλέγω, light up, rekindle.

ἀν-έρχομαι, go up, return.

ἀν-έχω, hold up, lift.

ἀν-ήρ, -δρός, ὁ, man, husband, warrior.

ἄνθρωπ-ος, -ου, ὁ, man, human being.

ἀν-οίγνῡμι and ἀν-οίγω, open.

ἄν-οικτ-ος, -ον, pitiless.

ἀν-οίκτως, without being pitied.

ἀν-ολολύζω, ἀν-ωλόλυξα, cry aloud.

ἀντ-αλλάσσω, ἀντ-ήλλαξα, give in exchange, give instead.

ἀντ-αμείβομαι, answer again.

ἀντ-έχομαι, with gen., grasp.

ἀντί, prep. with gen., instead of.

ἀντί-παλ-ος, -ον, wrestling against, rivalling.

ἀντι-πορθέω, ravage in return.

ἀντι-τίθημι, ἀντ-έθηκα, set against.

ἄνω, adv., above.

ἄξι-ος, -α, -ον, with gen., worthy.

ἀοιδ-ή, -ῆς, ἡ, song.

ἀοιδ-ός, -οῦ, ὁ and ἡ, singer.

ἀπ-άγω, bring away.

ἀπ-αίρω, ἀπ-ῆρα, sail away.

ἄπαις, ἄπαιδος, ὁ, ἡ, adj., childless.

ἀπ-αλλάσσω, ἀπ-ήλλαξα, ἀπ-ηλλάχθην, set free.

ἄπᾶς, ἄπᾶσα, ἄπᾶν, all, all together.

ἄπ-ειμι be away, be absent.

ἀπ-εμπολάω, sell, betray.

ἀπήν-η, -ης, ἡ, vehicle, chariot.

ἀπό, prep. with gen., from.

ἀπο-δίδωμι, ἀπ-έδωκα, repay, atone for.

ἀπο-κτείνω, ἀπο-κτενῶ, ἀπ-έκτεινα, kill.

ἄπολ-ις, -ι, having no city, being no city.

ἀπ-όλλῡμι, destroy.

ἀπο-νίζω, ἀπ-ένιψα, wash clean.

ἀπορ-ρήγνῡμι, ἀπορ-ρήξω, break off, tear away.

ἀπο-σκυθίζω, shave bare.
ἀπο-στέλλομαι, depart.
ἀπο-στερέω, rob, defraud.
ἀπο-φθείρω, aor. pass. ἀπ-εφθάρην, destroy.
ἄρα, unemphatic particle, then, there.
ἀρ-ά, -ᾶς, ἡ, curse.
ἀράσσω, beat, strike.
Ἄργει-ος, -α, -ον, Argive, Greek.
ἀργέω, be idle.
ἀρήγω, ward off.
ἄρθρ-ον, -ου, τό, joint, socket.
Ἀρκ-άς, -άδος, ὁ, adj., Arcadian.
ἁρμόζω, ἥρμοσα, join, fit.
ἁρπάζω, seize.
ἀρχ-ή, -ῆς, ἡ, beginning, origin.
ἀρχηγέτ-ης, -ου, ὁ, leader, chief.
ἀρχηγ-ός, -οῦ, ὁ, leader.
ἄρχομαι, begin.
ἄρχω, with gen., begin.
Ἀσιατ-ίς, -ίδος, ἡ, Asiatic woman.
ἀσκέω, dress up, deck.
ἄσμεν-ος, -η, -ον, rejoicing, glad.
ἀσπάζομαι, greet, kiss.
ἄσπασμ-α, -ατος, τό, embrace.
ἄσπετ-ος, -ον, unutterable.
ἀσπ-ίς, -ίδος, ἡ, shield.
ἄστρ-ον, -ου, τό, star.
ἄστ-υ, -εως, τό, city.
ἀτάρ, but.
ἄτεκν-ος, -ον, childless.
ἄτ-η, -ης, ἡ, blind infatuation, reckless guilt, ruin.
ἄττα, see τις.
αὖ, again, further, moreover.
αὐγ-ή, -ῆς, ἡ, dawn.
αὐδάω, speak, say, order.
αὐδ-ή, -ῆς, ἡ, voice, utterance.
αὖθις, again.
αὔρ-α, -ας, ἡ, breeze.
αὐτ-ός, -ή, -ό, (1) emphatic pron.,

myself, himself, etc. (2) oblique cases, him, her, it, etc. (3) after the article, the same.
αὐτοῦ, adv. here. See 716, note.
αὐχέω, boast, declare.
ἀφ-αιρέω, ἀφ-εῖλον, take away; mid., prevent; pass., be robbed.
ἀφαν-ής, -ές, unseen, disappeared.
ἀφ-ίημι, ἀφ-ῆκα, send forth.
ἀφ-ικνέομαι, ἀφ-ικόμην, arrive.
ἄφιλ-ος, -ον, friendless.
ἀφ-ίστημι, intrans. aor. ἀπ-έστην, remove, cause to stand away or revolt.
ἀφ-ορμάω, depart.
ἀφροσύν-η, -ης, ἡ, folly.
Ἀχαι-ός, -ά, -όν, Achaean, Greek.
Ἀχιλλ-εύς, -έως, ὁ, Achilles.
ἄψοφ-ος, -ον, noiseless.

B

βάθ-ος, -ους, τό, depth.
βάθρ-ον, -ου, τό, base, step, foundation.
βαίνω, ἔβην, βέβηκα, step, go, set one's feet.
βάκτρ-ον, -ου, τό, stick.
βάκχευμ-α, -ατος, τό, Bacchic orgy or revelry.
βακχεύω, take part in Bacchic celebration.
βάλλω, βαλῶ, ἔβαλον, throw, strike. See 1137, note.
βάρβαρ-ος, -ον, un-Greek, foreign.
βασίλει-α, -ας, ἡ, queen.
βασιλεί-ᾱ, -ας, ἡ, kingdom.
βασιλικ-ός, -ή, -όν, royal.
βάσ-ις, -εως, ἡ, step, foot, base.
βέβαι-ος, -α, -ον and βέβαι-ος, -ον, sure, certain.

βῆμ-α, -ατος, τό, step, pace, platform.

βί-α, -ας, ἡ, violence.

βιαίως, violently.

βί-ος, -ου, ὁ, life.

βλέπω, ἔβλεψα, see.

βλώσκω, ἔμολον, come.

βοάω, shout, cry, re-echo.

βο-ή, -ῆς, ἡ, shout, cry.

βολ-ή, -ῆς, ἡ, cast, stroke, ray.

βόστρυχ-ος, -ου, ὁ, curl.

βου-θυτέω, sacrifice oxen.

βούλευμ-α, -ατος, τό, resolution, purpose.

βούλομαι, wish, be willing.

βραχ-ύς, -εῖα, -ύ, short, small.

βρέμω, roar, clash.

βρέτ-ας, -εος, τό, wooden image.

βρέφ-ος, -ους, τό, baby.

βρῖθ-ος, -ους, τό, weight.

βροτ-ός, -οῦ, ὁ, mortal man.

βωμ-ός, -οῦ, ὁ, altar.

Γ

γαῖ-α, -ας, ἡ, earth.

γαμέτ-ης, -ου, ὁ, bridegroom, husband.

γαμέω, fut. γαμέω, ἔγημα, ἐγάμην, marry.

γαμήλι-ος, -ον, nuptial.

γάμ-ος, -ου, ὁ, wedding, marriage.

γάρ, conj., for.

γαύρωμ-α, -ατος, τό, subject for boasting.

γε, enclitic particle, at least, of course.

γέλ-ως, -ωτος, ὁ, laughter.

γένν-α, -ης, ἡ, race.

γέν-ος, -ους, τό, race, kind.

γεραι-ά, -ᾶς, ἡ, old woman.

γεραι-ός, -ά, -όν, old.

γέρ-ας, -αος, τό, gift of honour.

γῆ, γῆς, ἡ, earth.

γίγνομαι, γενήσομαι, ἐγενόμην, become, happen.

γιγνώσκω, ἔγνων, perf. pass. ἔγνωσμαι, learn, get to know.

γλῶσσ-α,-ης, ἡ, tongue, language.

γνώμ-η, -ης, ἡ, thoughts, inclination.

γοάω, weep, bewail.

γόν-ος, -ου, ὁ, child, race.

γόν-υ, -ατος, τό, knee.

γό-ος, -ου, ὁ, weeping, wailing.

γραῦς, γρᾱός, ἡ, old woman.

γράφω, ἔγραψα, write.

γυμν-άς, -άδος, fem. adj., naked.

γυν-ή, -αικός, ἡ, woman, wife.

Δ

δᾳδουχέω, hold the torch.

δαίμ-ων, -ονος, ὁ, god.

δαίνυμαι, feast on.

δάκ-ος, -ους, τό, noxious beast.

δάκρυ and δάκρυ-ον, -ου , τό, tear.

δακρύω, weep, weep for.

δᾱλ-ός, -οῦ, ὁ, torch.

δάμ-αρ, -αρτος, ἡ, wife.

Δαναΐδ-αι, -ῶν, οἱ, sons of Danaus (Greeks).

δαπάν-η, -ης, ἡ, cost, expense, extravagance.

δάπεδ-ον, -ου, τό, floor, ground.

δατέομαι, ἐδασάμην, divide.

δάφν-η, -ης, ἡ, laurel, bay.

δέ, but, and.

δεῖ με, I must.

δείδω, ἔδεισα, δέδοικα, fear.

δείκνῡμι, δείξω, show.

δειν-ός, -ή, -όν, terrible.

δεκάσπορ-ος, -ου, ὁ. See 20, note.

δέμας, τό, indecl., body.

δέμνι-ον, -ου, τό, bed.

δέομαι with gen., need.

δέρκομαι, *perf.* δέδορκα, see. See 707, *note.*

δεσπόζω, rule, master.

δεσπότ-ης, -ου, ὁ, master.

δεύομαι, *as* δέομαι.

δεῦρο, hither.

δεύτερον, secondly.

δέχομαι, δέξομαι, ἐδεξάμην, receive.

δή, *particle*, indeed, then.

Δήλι-ος, -ον, *adj.*, of the island of Delos.

δήποτε, once, formerly.

δῆτα, indeed. τί δῆτα; Why then?

διά, *prep. with gen.*, because of; *with acc.*, through. See 758, *note.*

δια-περάω, go across.

δια-φέρει, *impers.*, it makes a difference.

δια-φθείρω, destroy.

διδάσκαλ-ος, -ου, ὁ, teacher.

δίδωμι, δώσω, ἔδωκα, δέδωκα, give.

δίδωμι δίκην, pay the penalty, be punished.

δι-εξ-έρχομαι, go through.

δι-εργάζομαι, δι-ειργασάμην, work out.

δι-ερέσσω, wave about.

δικαίως, justly.

δίκ-η, -ης, ἡ, justice. See δίδωμι.

δίν-η, -ης, ἡ, whirlwind, eddy.

δι-όλλῡμι, *perf. intrans.* δι-όλωλα, destroy; *intrans.*, perish.

δίπτυχ-ος, -ον, double, two-fold.

δμώς, δμωός, ὁ, slave.

δνοφώδ-ης, -ες, dark.

δοκέω, ἔδοξα, think, seem. See 713, *note.*

δόλι-ος, -α, -ον *and* δόλι-ος, -ον, deceitful, treacherous.

δόμ-ος, -ου, ὁ, house, family.

δοξάζω, think, suppose.

δοριάλωτ-ος, -ον, captured by the spear.

δοριθήρᾱτ-ος, -ον, captured by the spear.

δόρυ, δορός *and* δόρατος, τό, spear-shaft, spear; 1148, mast.

δόσ-ις, -εως, ἡ, gift. See 925, *note.*

δουλεύω, be a slave, serve.

δούλ-η, -ης, ἡ, slave.

δοῦλ-ος, -ου, ὁ, slave.

Δούρει-ος, -α, -ον, wooden. See 14, *note.*

δράσσομαι, *with gen.*, clutch.

δράω, do. κακῶς δράω, do wrong to.

δρομ-άς, -άδος, ὁ, ἡ, running, frenzied.

δρόμ-ος, -ου, ὁ, course, race, running.

δύναμαι, be able.

δύναμ-ις, -εως, ἡ, power, strength.

δύο, δυοῖν, οἱ, αἱ, τά, two.

δυσλόφως, impatiently.

δύσνοστ-ος, -ον, ill-returning.

δύσποτμ-ος, -ον, ill-fated.

δύστην-ος, -ον, unfortunate.

δυστόπαστ-ος, -ον, hard to guess.

δυστυχ-ής, -ές, unhappy.

δυσχερ-ής, -ές, difficult, unpleasant.

δωρέομαι, give.

δῶρ-ον, -ου, τό, gift.

E

ἒ ἔ, *interj. of pain or grief.*

ἔᾱ, *interj. of surprise or displeasure.*

ἐάν, *conj. with subjunctive*, if.

ἑαυτ-όν, -ήν, -ό, *reflexive pron.*, oneself.

ἐάω, allow, let alone. *See* 877, *note.*

ἐγ-καθ-υβρίζω, revel in.

ἐγκύμ-ων, -ον, *gen.* -ονος, pregnant.

ἕδρ-α, -ας, ἡ, seat, resting-place.

ἕδραν-ον, -ου, τό, dwelling-place.

ἐθέλω, *as* θέλω.

εἰ, *conj.*, if.

εἷα, *interj.*, away!

εἶδ-ος, -ους, τό, form, beauty.

εἶέν, *particle*, well then!

εἰκ-ώ, -οῦς, ἡ, image, semblance.

εἰμί, be.

εἶμι, go; *used as fut. of* ἔρχομαι.

εἰρεσί-α, -ας, ἡ, oarage. *See* 570, *note.*

εἰς, ἐς, *prep. with acc.*, into, to.

εἷς, μία, ἕν, one.

εἰσ-οράω, εἰσεῖδον, look at, behold.

εἰσ-πίπτω, fall into, fall upon.

εἰσ-φρέω, let in, admit.

εἶτα, then, next.

εἴτε . . . εἴτε, whether . . . or.

ἐκ, ἐξ, ἐχ, *prep. with gen.*, out of, from.

ἕκαστ-ος, -η, -ον, each, every.

ἐκ-βαίνω, step out, turn out.

ἐκ-βάλλω, *perf.* ἐκ-βέβληκα, *perf. pass.* ἐκ-βέβλημαι, cast out, utter.

ἐκ-γελάω, laugh aloud, gurgle out.

ἐκεῖ, there.

ἐκεῖθεν, thence.

ἐκεῖν-ος, -η, -ο, *demonstrative adj. and pron.*, that; he, she, it.

ἐκεῖσε, thither.

ἐκ-κομίζω, bring out, take away.

ἔκκριτον, *adv.*, above all.

ἐκ-λείπω, *perf.* ἐκ-λέλοιπα, leave out, abandon.

ἔκλυτ-ος, -ον, loose, relaxed.

ἐκ-μαργόομαι, *aor.* ἐξ-εμαργώθην, go raving mad.

ἐκ-μοχθέω, achieve by struggle.

ἑκούσι-ος, -α, -ον *and* ἑκούσι-ος, -ον, willing, acting voluntarily.

ἐκ-παγλέομαι, be struck with wonder at.

ἐκ-πέμπω, send out.

ἐκ-πορθέω, plunder, carry off.

ἐκπρεπ-ής, -ές, distinguished among all.

ἐκ-πυρόω, burn to ashes.

ἐκ-τρέφω, ἐξ-έθρεψα, nourish, rear.

ἐκ-φύω, ἐξ-έφυσα, beget, produce. *See* 767, *note.*

ἐκ-ών, -οῦσα, -όν, *gen.* ἑκόντος, willing.

ἐλεύθερ-ος, -α, -ον, free.

ἐλίσσω, wind.

ἕλκ-ος, -ους, τό, wound.

ἕλκω, drag, draw, tear.

Ἑλλ-άς, -άδος, ἡ, Greece.

Ἕλλ-ην, -ηνος, ὁ, *adj. and noun*, Greek.

Ἑλληνικ-ός, -ή, -όν, Greek.

ἐλπίζω, hope, expect.

ἐλπ-ίς, -ίδος, ἡ, hope.

ἐμ-βαίνω, step in, embark.

ἐμ-βάλλω, throw in, put in, inflict.

ἐμ-ός, -ή, -όν, my, mine.

ἐμ-πίμπρημι, set on fire. .

ἔμπληκτ-ος, -ον, stupid, capricious.

ἐν, *prep. with dat.*, in, among.

ἐναντί-ος, -α, -ον, opposite, opposing.

ἐνδε-ής, -ές, *with gen.*, lacking, without.

ἔνδικ-ος, -ον, right, just.

ἔνδον, adv., within.
ἐνδυτ-ός, -όν, worn; clothed.
ἐνέπω, tell, speak.
ἔνερθε, adv. with gen., below.
ἔνθα, where, relative.
ἐνθάδε, here.
ἔνθεν, hence, hereafter.
ἐνθένδε, after that.
ἔνθε-ος, -ον, possessed by a god.
ἐνθουσιάζω, be possessed by a
   god.
ἐν-ίημι, perf. pass. ἐν-είμην,
   throw in.
ἔνοπλ-ος, -ον, having arms within.
ἐντός, prep. with gen., within.
ἐξ, as ἐκ.
ἐξ-άγω, lead from.
ἐξαίρετ-ος, -ον, chosen.
ἐξ-αιρέω, remove, destroy.
ἐξ-αιτέω, demand.
ἐξ-ακοντίζω, shout forth, proclaim aloud.
ἐξ-αν-έρχομαι, ἐξ-αν-ῆλθον, come
   forth from.
ἐξ-αν-ίστημι, destroy.
ἐξ-ανύω, accomplish.
ἐξ-απ-όλλυμι, ἐξ-απ-ώλεσα, destroy
   utterly.
ἐξ-άπτω, fasten to, place upon.
ἐξαρκέω, suffice. See 653, note.
ἔξ-ειμι, ἐξ-ιέναι, go out.
ἐξ-ελίσσω, unwind, weave.
ἐξ-έρχομαι, go out, come out.
ἔξ-εστί μοι, impers., it is
   allowed to me, I may.
ἐξ-ευρίσκω, ἐξ-εῦρον, find out.
ἐξ-ίημι, throw out. See 94, note.
ἐξ-ορμάω, set out from.
ἔξω, adv. with gen., outside. See
   345, note.
ἑορτ-ή, -ῆς, ἡ, feast, festival.
ἐπαινέω, praise, approve.

ἔπαιν-ος, -ου, ὁ, praise.
ἐπ-αμπ-έχω, put on over.
ἐπ-άξι-ος, -α, -ον, with gen., worthy.
ἐπεί, when, since, because.
ἐπί, prep. with gen., on. See 74,
   327, notes. With dat., after,
   following upon. See 315, 945,
   1022, notes.
ἐπίγραμμ-α, -ατος, τό, epitaph.
ἐπικήδει-ος, -ον, of a funeral.
ἐπί-λοιπ-ος, -ον, remaining.
ἐπι-σπάω, drag after one.
ἐπι-σπεύδω, hasten onward.
ἐπι-στέλλω, perf. pass. ἐπ-έσταλμαι,
   command.
ἐπι-στρατεύω, make war upon.
ἐπίφθον-ος, -ον, envious, odious.
ἕπομαι, ἑσπόμην, with dat., follow, accompany.
ἔπ-ος, -ους, τό, word, saying.
ἐραστ-ής, -οῦ, ὁ, lover.
ἐράω, with gen., love.
ἔργ-ον, -ου, τό, deed, work.
ἐρείπι-α, -ων, τά, wreckage, frag-
   ments.
ἐρημί-α, -ας, ἡ, desolation.
ἔρημ-ος, -η, -ον, desolate, solitary;
   with gen., bereft of.
Ἐρῖν-ύς, -ύος, ἡ, avenging deity;
   guilt.
ἑρκεῖ-ος, -α, -ον and ἑρκεῖ-ος, -ον,
   of the fore-court.
ἔρν-ος, -ους, τό, shoot, offspring.
ἕρπω, go, come.
ἔρχομαι, εἶμι, ἦλθον, ἐλήλυθα, go,
   come.
ἔρ-ως, -ωτος, ὁ, love, desire.
ἐρωτάω, ἐρήσομαι, ἠρόμην, ask.
ἐς, as εἰς.
ἐσ-βαίνω, ἐσ-βήσομαι, ἐσ-έβην, go
   into, embark.
ἔσθημ-α, -ατος, τό, garment.

ἐσθλ-ός, -ή, -όν, good, brave.

ἑστί-α, -ας, ἡ, hearth, home.

ἐσ-φέρω, bring in, bring upon.

ἔσω, adv. with gen., inside.

ἕτερ-ος, -α, -ον, the other, different.

ἔτι, yet, still.

ἕτοιμ-ος, -ον, ready.

εὖ, adv., well.

εὐάν, a cry of the Bacchanals.

εὐγένει-α, -ας, ἡ, nobility.

εὐγεν-ής, -ές, noble, well-born.

εὐδαιμονίζω, call happy.

εὐδαίμ-ων, -ον, gen. -ονος, happy, fortunate.

εὐδοξί-α, -ας, ἡ, good repute.

εὔι-ος, -ον, Bacchic.

εὐμορφί-α, -ας, ἡ, beauty.

εὐν-ή, -ῆς, ἡ, bed.

εὔνοι-α, -ας, ἡ, goodwill, favour.

εὐοῖ, a cry of the Bacchanals.

εὐπραξί-α, -ας, ἡ, happiness.

εὑρίσκω, εὗρον and ηὗρον, perf. pass. εὕρημαι and ηὕρημαι, find.

εὐσεβέω, act reverently.

εὐσεβ-ής, -ές, reverent, dutiful, pious.

εὐτυχέω, be fortunate, be successful.

εὐτυχ-ής, -ές, fortunate.

εὐφραίνω, εὔφρᾱνα, make glad.

εὔ-φρων, -φρον, gen. -φρονος, glad, cheerful.

εὐχ-ή, -ῆς, ἡ, prayer.

ἐφ-έλκω, drag after; mid., bring on, cause.

ἐχ, as ἐκ.

ἐχθρ-ός, -οῦ, ὁ, enemy.

ἐχθρ-ός, -ά, -όν, hateful; hating.

ἔχω, ἕξω, ἔσχον, imperf. εἶχον, have, keep, keep on. See 268, 317, 923, notes.

Z

ζάθε-ος, -α, -ον and ζάθε-ος, -ον, very divine, sacred.

ζάω, infin. ζῆν, live.

ζεύγνῡμι, yoke, join.

ζεῦγ-ος, -ους, τό, yoke, pair, team. See 924, note.

ζω-ή, -ῆς, ἡ, life.

Η

ἤ, interrog. particle.

ἦ, in truth.

ἤ, than. ἤ . . . ἤ, ? . . . or?

ἥβ-η, -ης, ἡ, youth, prime of youth.

ἡγέομαι, think, consider.

ἡδέως, gladly, willingly.

ἤδη, now, already.

ἡδον-ή, -ῆς, ἡ, pleasure.

ἡδ-ύς, -εῖα, -ύ, sweet, pleasant.

ἥκω, I am here, I have come.

ἥλι-ος, -ου, ὁ, sun.

ἦμ-αρ, -ατος, τό, day.

ἡμέρ-α, -ας, ἡ, day.

ἡμέτερ-ος, -α, -ον, our.

ἡνίκα, when; 70, that.

ἤπι-ος, -α, -ον and ἤπι-ος, -ον, gentle, kindly.

Ἥρ-α, -ας, ἡ, the goddess Hera, wife of Zeus.

ἥσυχ-ος, -ον, quiet.

ἠχ-ώ, -οῦς, ἡ, echo, sound.

Θ

θάλαμ-ος, -ου, ὁ, marriage-chamber.

θάνατ-ος, -ου, ὁ, death.

θάπτω, ἔθαψα, aor. pass. ἐτάφην, bury.

θέ-α, -ας, ἡ, spectacle, seeing.

θε-ά, -ᾶς, ἡ, goddess.

θέᾱμ-α, -ατος, τό, sight, spectacle.

θέλω, wish, be willing. *See* 27, *note*.

θε-ός, -οῦ, ὁ *and* ἡ, god, goddess.

θεοστυγ-ής, -ές, hated by the gods.

θέσμι-ον, -ον, τό, law, custom, rite.

Θεσσαλ-ός, -ή, -όν, Thessalian.

θῆλ-υς, -εια, -υ, female.

θήρ, θηρός, ὁ, wild beast.

θηράω, hunt, pursue, seek.

Θησεῖδ-αι, -ῶν, οἱ, the sons of Theseus; Athenians.

θιγγάνω, ἔθιγον, *with gen.*, touch.

θνήσκω, θανέομαι, ἔθανον, τέθνηκα, die.

θνητ-ός, -ή, -όν, mortal.

θοάζω, hurry, rush.

θο-ός, -ή, -όν, swift.

θροέω, cry out, utter aloud.

θυηπολέω, sacrifice.

I

ἴακχ-ος, -ον, ὁ, song, chorus.

ἰάομαι, heal, treat.

ἰᾱτρ-ός, -οῦ, ὁ, healer.

ἰαχέω, wail, cry, shout.

ἰαχ-ή, -ῆς, ἡ, cry, shout.

ἰδού, *interj.*, behold!

ἱερ-όν, -οῦ, τό, temple, holy place.

ἱερ-ός, -ά, -όν *and* ἱερ-ός, -όν, holy.

ἱκαν-ός, -ή, -όν, sufficient.

'Ιλι-άς, -άδος, *fem. adj.*, Trojan.

ἵνα, *conj.*, in order that.

ἴνις, ὁ, son.

ἵππ-ος, -ου, ὁ, horse.

ἰσόθε-ος, -ον, equal to the gods, godlike.

ἴσ-ος, -η, -ον, equal, fair.

ἵστημι, *fut. mid.* στήσομαι, *aor. pass.* ἐστάθην, set up, stand.

ἱστί-ον, -ου, cloth, sail.

ἱστορέω, ask, inquire.

ἰσχ-ύς, -ύος, ἡ, strength.

ἰσχύω, be strong.

ἴσως, perhaps.

ἰτέ-α, -ας, ἡ, willow.

ἴχν-ος, -ους, τό, track, trace.

ἰώ, *interj*.

K

καί, and, also, even.

καινίζω, make new, make strange. *See* 889, *note*.

καιν-ός, -ή, -όν, new.

καιρ-ός, -οῦ, ὁ, time, opportunity. *See* 744, *note*.

κακ-ός, -ή, -όν, evil, bad.

κακοῦργ-ος, -ον, villainous, criminal.

καλέω, *fut. perf. pass.* κεκλήσομαι, call.

καλλίνικ-ος, -ον, gloriously triumphant.

καλλίπεπλ-ος, -ον, with fair robe.

καλλιφεγγ-ής, -ές, beautifully shining.

καλλον-ή, -ῆς, ἡ, beauty.

κάλλ-ος, -ους, τό, beauty.

καλ-ός, -ή, -όν, *superl.* κάλλιστος, good, beautiful.

κάλ-ως, -ω, ὁ, rope, cable.

κάμνω, *perf.* κέκμηκα, work, toil, do. *See* 96, *note*.

καν-ών, -όνος, ὁ, straight rod, rule, standard.

καπνόω, turn to smoke.

κάρᾱ, τό, *irreg.* head.

καραδοκέω, await the outcome. *See* 93, 456, *notes*.

καράτομ-ος, -ον, beheading. *See* 564, *note*.

κάρτα, very, surely.

κατά, prep. with acc., according to, throughout, in, among; with gen., against. See 76, 244, notes.

κατα-θνήσκω, κατ-έθανον, die.

κατ-αιθαλόω, burn to ashes.

κατ-αισχύνω, disgrace.

κατα-κλύζω, flood, overflow.

κατα-κνάπτω, κατ-έκναψα, tear to pieces.

κατα-ξαίνω, aor. pass. κατ-εξάνθην, tear to pieces, waste away.

κατάπτυστ-ος, -ον, fit to be spat on.

κατ-αριθμέω, count.

καταρ-ρέω, flow down, drip.

κατα-σκάπτω, dig down, destroy utterly.

κατα-στένω, lament.

κατ-έχω, imperf. κατ-εῖχον, possess, fill.

κατ-ηγορέω, with gen., accuse.

κάτ-οιδα, know well, understand.

Καφήρει-ος, -ον, see note.

κέδρ-ος, -ου, ἡ, cedar.

κεῖμαι, lie.

κείρω, κερῶ, ἔκειρα, cut.

κελαιν-ός, -ή, -όν, black, dark.

κέλευθ-ος, -ου, ἡ, road, path.

κεν-ός, -ή, -όν, empty. See 758, note.

κεραύνι-ος, -ον, of a thunderbolt.

κήλημ-α, -ατος, -τό, spell, charm.

κηπεύω, tend, cherish.

κήρ, κηρός, ἡ, doom, 'plague, ruin.

κηρ ῡκεύω, proclaim, announce.

κήρ-υξ, -ῡκος, ὁ, herald, messenger.

κλειν-ός, -ή, -όν, famous.

κλέος, -τό, report, fame.

κλῆρ-ος, -ου, ὁ, lot, drawing of lots.

κληρόω, allot; mid., obtain by lot.

κλήϊς, κληδός, ἡ, garland. See 256, note.

κλύω, with acc. and gen., hear.

κλωστ-ός, -ή, -όν, spun.

κνέφ-ας, -ους, τό, darkness.

κοῖλ-ος, -η, -ον, hollow, empty.

κοιν-ός, -ή, -όν, common, shared.

κοινόω, make common, share.

κολάζω, chastise, punish.

κόμ-η, -ης, ἡ, hair.

κομίζω, bring.

κόμπ-ος, -ου, ὁ, boast.

κομψ-ός, -ή, -όν, refined, fine, witty. See 651, note.

κόρ-η, -ης, ἡ, girl, maiden, daughter.

κορυφ-ή, -ῆς, ἡ, summit, height.

κοσμέω, deck out, adorn, honour.

κόσμ-ος, -ου, ὁ, adornment.

κούριμ-ος, -η, -ον, shorn.

κουροτρόφ-ος, -ον, rearing children.

κοῦφ-ος, -η, -ον, light, unsubstantial.

κραίνω, aor. pass. ἐκράνθην, accomplish, ordain.

κράς, κρατός, τό, head.

κρᾶτα, τό, indecl., head.

κρατέω, with gen., rule, master; with acc., conquer.

κράτ-ος, -ους, τό, power, rule.

κρήδεμν-ον, -ου, τό, head-dress; pl., battlements.

κρηπῑ-ίς, -ῖδος, ἡ, pedestal, foundation.

κρίνω, ἔκρῑνα, judge. See 928, note.

κρότ-ος, -ου, ὁ, noise, beat.

κρυπτ-ός, -ή, -όν, hidden, secret.

κρύπτω, hide.

G

κτάομαι, *perf.* κέκτημαι, get, receive; *perf.*, possess.

κτείνω, κτενῶ, ἔκτανον *and* ἔκτεινα, kill.

κτερίσματ-α, -ων, τά, funeral gifts.

κτυπέω, crash, make resound, resound.

Κύπρ-ις, -ιδος, ἡ, Aphrodite, love.

κωκῡτ-ός, -οῦ, ὁ, wailing.

κῶμ-ος, -ου, ὁ, band, company.

Λ

λαγχάνω, λήξομαι, ἔλαχον, εἴληχα *and* λέλογχα, ἐλήχθην, εἴληγμαι, *with acc. and gen.*, obtain by lot, get.

λάθρᾱ, secretly.

λάϊν-ος, -η, -ον, of stone.

Λάκαιν-α, -ης, ἡ, Spartan woman.

λαμβάνω, λήψομαι, ἔλαβον, take, receive.

λαμπ-άς, -άδος, ἡ, torch.

λαμπρ-ός, -ά, -όν, bright, shining.

λάσκω, ἔλακον, scream, cry, shriek.

λάτρ-ις, -ιος, ὁ *and* ἡ, servant.

λάφῡρ-α, -ων, τά, spoils of war.

λέγω, λέξω, ἔλεξα *and* εἶπον, say, speak.

λείπω, ἔλιπον, *perf. pass.* λέλειμμαι, leave behind.

λείψαν-ον, -ου, τό, remnant.

λέκτρ-ον, -ου, τό, bed.

λεύσσω, see.

λευστ-ήρ, -ῆρος, ὁ, stone-thrower.

λέχ-ος, -ους, τό, bed, marriage.

λε-ώς, -ώ, ὁ, people, host.

ληΐζομαι *and* ληΐζω, *perf. pass.* λέλησμαι, carry off, plunder.

λίαν, *adv.*, very, too much.

Λίβ-υς, -υος, ὁ, Libyan.

λίν-ον, -ου, τό, flax, thread.

λίσσομαι, beseech.

λόγ-ος, -ου, ὁ, word, tale, argument.

λοιπ-ός, -ή, -όν, remaining. *See* 85, *note.*

λοίσθι-ος, -α, -ον, last.

Λοξί-ᾱς, -ου, ὁ, Apollo, god of the sun and of oracles.

λούω, wash, bathe.

λοχαγ-ός, -οῦ, ὁ, captain.

λόχ-ος, -ου, ὁ, ambush, hiding-place.

λυγρ-ός, -ά, -όν, baneful, mournful.

λύπ-η, -ης, ἡ, grief.

λυπρ-ός, -ά, -όν, sorrowful.

λύω, unbind, release, relax.

λωτ-ός, -οῦ, ὁ, flute.

Μ

μαιν-άς, -άδος, ἡ, frenzied, mad.

μακάρι-ος, -α, -ον, blessed, happy.

μακρ-ός, -ά, -όν, long, great. *See* 460, *note.*

μάλα, *adv.*, very, very much.

μάλιστα, *superl. of* μάλα, yes, certainly.

μᾶλλον, *compar. of* μάλα, more.

μανθάνω, learn, get to know.

μαντεῖ-ος, -α, -ον *and* μαντεῖ-ος, -ον, prophetic.

μάρναμαι, fight.

μαστ-ός, -οῦ, ὁ, breast.

μάτην, *adv.*, in vain.

μάχ-η, -ης, ἡ, battle, fight.

μέγας, μεγάλη, μέγα, great.

μεθ-ήκω, come in search of. *See* ἥκω.

μεθ-ίημι, *aor.* μεθ-ῆκα, throw, let go, let fall; leave.

μέλαθρ-ον, -ου, τό, house.

μέλας, μέλαινα, μέλαν, black, dark.

μέλε-ος, -α, -ον, unhappy.

μέλλω, be about to, be destined to.

μέλ-ος, -ους, τό, limb; song.

μέλπω, sing.

μέν . . . δέ, particles showing contrast.

μένω, wait, await.

μέσ-ος, -η, -ον, middle. ἐς μέσον, into the middle, into the open.

μετά, prep. with gen., with, together with.

μέτρι-ος, -α, -ον, within measure, moderate.

μή, lest. εἰ μή, if not.

μηδαμοῦ, nowhere, by no means.

μηδέ,, and . . . not.

μηδ-είς, -εμία, -έν, no one.

μηκέτι, no longer.

μήν, particle, truly. καὶ μήν, introducing a new character on the stage, or a new argument.

μήτε . . . μήτε, neither . . . nor.

μητροκτόν-ος, -ον, killing one's mother.

μηχαν-ή, -ῆς, ἡ, device, machine.

μιαιφόν-ος, -ον, murderous.

μῑκρ-ός, -ά, -όν, small. See 1040, note.

μίμημ-α, -ατος, τό, imitation.

μίμνω, wait, await.

μισέω, hate.

μνῆμ-α, -ατος, τό, remembrance, memorial.

μογερ-ός, -ά, -όν, troublesome, wretched.

μον-ή, -ῆς, ἡ, act of remaining.

μόρ-ος, -ου, ὁ, fate, death.

μορφ-ή, -ῆς, ἡ, shape, form, beauty.

μοῦσ-α, -ης, ἡ, muse, music.

μουσοποι-ός, -οῦ, ὁ, poet.

μοχθέω, toil, labour.

μόχθ-ος, -ου, ὁ, labour.

μῦθ-ος, -ου, ὁ, word, speech, tale.

μυρί-ος, -α, -ον, numberless.

μυσαρ-ός, -ά, -όν, foul, loathsome.

μυχ-ός, -οῦ, ὁ, nook, corner, inmost part of the house.

μῶν, interrog. particle. See 714, note.

μῶρ-ος, -α, -ον and μωρ-ος, -ον, dull, stupid.

N

νᾱ-ός, -οῦ, ὁ, temple.

ναύπορ-ος, -ον, ship-speeding.

ναῦς, νεώς, ἡ, ship.

ναυστολέω, carry by sea.

νεᾱνί-ᾱς, -ου, ὁ, young man.

νεᾶν-ις, -ιδος, ἡ, young woman.

νεκρ-ός, -οῦ, ὁ, corpse.

νέκ-υς, -υος, ὁ, corpse.

νέ-ος, -α, -ον, young, new.

νεοσσ-ός, οῦ, ὁ, young bird, nestling.

νεοχμ-ός, -όν, new.

νέρτερ-ος, -α, -ον and νέρτερ-ος, -ον, lower. οἱ νέρτεροι, those below, the dead.

Νηρη-ΐς, -ΐδος, ἡ, daughter of Nereus, sea-nymph.

νῑκάω, conquer, prevail.

νίκ-η, -ης, ἡ, victory.

νῑκητήρι-ον, -ου, τό, prize of victory.

νῑκη-φόρ-ος, -ον, victorious, winning.

νιν, enclitic pron., him, her, them.

νομίζω, think, suppose.

νόμ-ος, -ου, ὁ, custom, law. See 324, note.

νοσέω, be ill.

νόσ-ος, -ου, ἡ, disease.

νόστ-ος, -ου, ὁ, return, home-coming.

νοῦς, νοῦ, ὁ, mind, heart, thoughts, intelligence.

νυμφευτήρι-ον, -ου, τό, marriage.

νυμφεύω, marry.

νύμφ-η, -ης, ἡ, bride.

νυμφί-ος, -ου, ὁ, bridegroom.

νύμφι-ος, -α, -ον, bridal, wedded.

νῦν, now.

νύχι-ος, -α, -ον and νύχι-ος, -ον, nightly, at night.

νῶτ-ος, -ου, ὁ and νῶτ-ον, -ου, τό, back, flat surface.

Ξ

ξεναπάτ-ης, -ου, ὁ, cheater of strangers, traitor.

ξενικ-ός, -ή, -όν, and ξενικ-ός, -όν, foreign, alien.

ξέν-ος, -ου, ὁ, stranger, foreigner, guest, host.

ξέν-ος, -η, -ον, strange, alien.

ξεστ-ός, -ή, -όν, hewn of timber, hewn of stone.

ξόαν-ον, -ου, τό, image.

ξύν, prep. with dat., with, with the help of. See σύν.

ξυν-αρμόζω, fit together.

O

ὄγκ-ος, -ου, ὁ, weight, pride.

ὅδε, ἥδε, τόδε, adj., this; pron., he, she, it.

ὁδ-ός, -οῦ, ἡ, road, way.

ὀδυρμ-α, -ατος, τό, wailing.

ὅθεν, relative, whence.

ὅθι, relative, where.

οἴ, interj. of grief.

οἵ, relative and indirect interrog., whither; 1029, how.

οἶδα, know.

οἴκαδε, homeward.

οἰκέω, live, inhabit.

οἴκοθεν, from home, at home, within oneself.

οἴκοι, at home.

οἶκ-ος, -ου, ὁ, home, house.

οἶκτ-ος, -ου, ὁ, pity.

οἶμαι, think, believe.

οἴμοι, interj. of pain, fright, grief, etc.

οἷ-ος, -α, -ον, relative, of what kind, such as, strong enough. See 732, note.

οἴχομαι, to have departed.

ὀλβίζω, think happy.

ὀλέθρι-ος, -α, -ον and ὀλέθρι-ος, -ον, deadly, ruinous.

ὄλεθρ-ος, -ου, ὁ, death, ruin.

ὄλλῡμι, ὤλεσα, destroy; mid. ὄλλυμαι, ὠλόμην, ὄλωλα, perish.

ὄμβρ-ος, -ου, ὁ, rain, storm.

ὁμῆλ-ιξ, -ικος, ὁ, ἡ, of the same age.

ὁμῑλί-α, -ας, ἡ, company, intercourse.

ὄμμ-α, -ατος, τό, eye, countenance.

ὅμοι-ος, -α, -ον, of like nature.

ὁμοίως, in like manner.

ὁμοῦ, together.

ὅμως, nevertheless.

ὀνειδίζω, reproach.

ὀνίνημι, ὤνησα, help, benefit.

ὄνομ-α, -ατος, τό, name.

ὄν-υξ, -υχος, ὁ, nail, claw, hoof.

ὀπᾰ-ων, -ονος, ὁ, attendant.

ὅπλ-α, -ων, τά, arms, weapons, gear.

ὅπως, relative and indirect interrog., as, how. ὅπως τάχιστα, as quickly as possible.

ὁράω, εἶδον, see.

ὀργ-ή, -ῆς, ἡ, temperament, mood, anger.

ὀρέστερ-ος, -α, -ον, of the mountains.

ὄρθι-ος, -α, -ον, shrill.

ὀρθ-ός, -ή, -όν, straight, upright, right.

ὀρθόω, set upright.

ὀρθῶς, rightly.

ὅρι-ον, -ου, τό, boundary, frontier.

ὁρμάω, start on the way.

ὅρ-ος, -ου, ὁ, boundary.

ὀρυκτ-ός, -ή, -όν, dug.

ὅς, ἥ, ὅ, relative pron., sometimes demonstrative.

ὅσι-ος, -α, -ον and ὅσι-ος, -ον, holy.

ὅσ-ος, -η, -ον, relative and indirect interrog., as great as, how great. ὅσ-οι, -αι, -α, as many as, how many.

ὅσπερ, ἥπερ, ὅπερ, relative pron., who, which.

ὀστέ-ον, -ου, τό, bone.

ὅστις, ἥτις, ὅτι, relative pron., who, whoever.

ὅταν, relative conj., when, whenever.

ὅτε, relative, when.

ὅτι, because; that (indirect statement).

οὗ, relative, where.

οὐ, οὐκ, οὐχ, not, no.

οὐδαμῇ, nowhere.

οὐδέ, and . . . not.

οὐδ-είς, -εμία, -έν, no one, nothing.

οὐκέτι, no longer.

οὖν, therefore, then, so.

οὕνεκα, with gen., because of.

οὔποτε, never.

οὔπω, not yet.

οὐράνι-ος, -α, -ον and οὐράνι-ος, -ον, of heaven. See 519, note.

οὐραν-ός, -οῦ, ὁ, heaven, sky.

οὔρει-ος, -η, -ον (Attic ὄρει-ος), of the mountains.

οὔρι-ος, -ον, favourable (describing wind).

οὖρ-ος, -ου, ὁ, fair wind.

οὔτε . . . οὔτε, neither . . . nor.

οὗτος, αὕτη, τοῦτο, this, this one.

οὕτως, thus.

οὐχί, as οὐ.

ὄχημ-α, -ατος, τό, that which upholds.

ὄχ-ος, -ου, ὁ, chariot.

Π

παιδι-ά, -ᾶς, ἡ, game, sport.

παῖς, παιδός, ὁ, ἡ, child.

πάλαι, long ago.

πάλιν, again, back.

Παλλ-άς, -άδος, ἡ, the goddess Pallas Athene.

πάλλω, poise, sway.

πάλ-ος, -ου, ὁ, lot, ballot.

παμφα-ής, -ές, all-shining.

παρά, prep. with gen., from; with dat., near.

παρα-δίδωμι, hand over, surrender.

παρα-λείπω, leave, neglect.

παρά-νομ-ος, -ον, lawless.

πάρεδρ-ος, -ον, sitting beside.

παρει-ά, -ᾶς, ἡ, cheek.

πάρ-ειμι, be at hand.

πάρ-εστί μοι, impers., I can, I may.

παρ-έχω, supply, offer, grant.

παρθενεί-α, -ας, ἡ, virginity.

παρθέν-ος, -ου, ἡ, maiden.

παρ-ίημι, give up, yield.

Παρνᾶσι-ος, -α, -ον, of Parnassus.

πάροιθε, before, formerly.

πάρος, *adv. and prep. with gen.*, before, instead of.

πᾶς, πᾶσα, πᾶν, all.

πάσχω, ἔπαθον, πέπονθα, suffer, feel, have something done to one.

πατ-ήρ, -ρός, ὁ, father.

πάτρ-α, -ας, ἡ, native land, city.

πατρ-ίς, -ίδος, ἡ, native land.

πατρῷ-ος, -α, -ον *and* πατρῷ-ος -ον, native, of one's father.

παύω, *perf. pass.* πέπαυμαι, stop.

πεδί-ον, -ου, τό, plain.

πέδ-ον, -ου, τό, ground, earth.

πείθω, ἔπεισα, persuade.

πειθ-ώ, -οῦς, ἡ, persuasion, persuasiveness.

πέλαγ-ος, -ους, τό, sea.

πέλας, *adv. with gen.*, near.

πέλεκ-υς, -εως, ὁ, axe.

πέμπω, send, send home, escort.

πένθ-ος, -ους, τό, grief.

πέπλ-ος, -ου, ὁ, dress, robe.

πεπρωμέν-ος, -η, -ον, destined.

πέρθω, ἔπερσα, ravage, destroy.

περί, *prep. with acc.*, around; *with gen.*, concerning.

περι-βάλλω, throw round, put round.

περιβολ-ή, -ῆς, ἡ, *as* περίβολος.

περίβολ-ος, -ου, ὁ, covering.

πέριξ, *adv.*, around.

περισσ-ός, -ή, -όν, remarkable, excessive.

περι-στέλλω, -έστειλα, -εστάλην, dress, wrap.

πέρνημι, *aor. pass.* ἐπράθην, sell, betray.

πέτρ-α, -ας, ἡ, rock, stone.

πέτριν-ος, -η, -ον, rocky, of rock.

πεύκ-η, -ης, ἡ, pine-tree, torch.

πηδάω, leap.

πήδημ-α, -ατος, τό, leap.

πικρ-ός, -ά, -όν, sharp, bitter.

πίμπλημι, fill.

πίμπρημι, burn, set fire to.

πίπτω, ἔπεσον, πέπτωκα, fall.

πίτυλ-ος, -ου, ὁ, stroke, sweep of the oars.

πλάτ-η, -ης, ἡ, oar-blade, oar.

πλευρ-όν, -οῦ, τό, rib, side.

πλήν, *prep. with gen.*, except.

πλησμον-ή, -ῆς, ἡ, satiety.

πλόκαμ-ος, -ου, ὁ, tress, lock.

πλούσι-ος, -α, -ον, rich.

πνεῦμ-α, -ατος, τό, breath, odour, spirit.

πνο-ή, -ῆς, ἡ, breath, wind.

πόθ-ος, -ου, ὁ, longing, love.

ποῖ, whither?

ποιέω, make, do, make out.

ποιν-ή, -ῆς, ἡ, penalty, vengeance.

ποῖ-ος, -α, -ον, of what sort?

πολέμι-ος, -ου, ὁ, enemy. πολέμι-ος, -α, -ον, hostile.

πόλ-ις, -εως, ἡ, city, country, state.

πολύς, πολλή, πολύ, much; *pl.*, many. *Compar.* πλείων, πλέον, more.

πολύσπορ-ος, -ον, of many crops, fruitful.

πόν-ος, -ου, ὁ, pain.

πόντ-ος, -ου, ὁ, sea.

πορεύω, carry, bring; *mid.*, go, journey.

πορθέω, ravage, destroy.

πορθμεύω, ferry, carry.

πόρ-ος, -ου, ὁ, way through, path, strait.

πόσ-ις, -ιος, ὁ, husband.

ποτέ, ever, at any time.

πότερον, *interrog. particle, introducing a double question. See* 978, *note.*

πότμ-ος, -ου, ὁ, destiny, doom.

πούς, ποδός, ὁ, foot. *See* 938, *note.*

πράσσω *and* πράττω, do, fare. εὖ πράσσω, be fortunate.

πρέσβ-υς, -εως, ὁ, old man.

πρευμν-ής, -ές, gentle.

Πρίαμ-ος, -ου, ὁ, Priam, king of Troy.

πρίν, *adv. and conj.,* before, formerly.

πρό, *prep. with gen.,* on behalf of, in defence of, in front of.

πρόγον-ος, -ου, ὁ, ancestor.

προ-δίδωμι, -έδωκα, betray.

πρόθ ῡμ-ος, -ον, willing, eager.

πρό-κειμαι, lie before, be set before.

πρόμ-ος, -ου, ὁ, chief.

προ-οίμι-ον, -ου, τό, beginning, introduction.

πρός, *prep. with acc.,* to, towards; *with gen.,* in the sight of; *with dat.,* at, near. See notes. *adv.,* besides.

πρόσ-ειμι (εἶναι), be at hand, belong to.

πρόσ-ειμι (ἰέναι), be added to.

προσ-εννέπω, address.

προσ-εύχομαι, pray to.

πρόσθεν, formerly.

προσ-κυνέω, worship, greet obsequiously.

προσ-πίπτω, embrace.

προσ-πολέω, attend, serve.

πρόσπολ-ος, -ου, ὁ *and* ἡ, attendant, servant.

πρόσπτυγμ-α, -ατος, τό, embrace.

προσ-τίθημι, -έθηκα, *aor. mid.* -εθέμην, give, put on, put to, impute to.

πρόσφθεγμ-α, -ατος, τό, salutation.

πρόσφορ-ος, -ον, useful, suitable.

προσφωνέω, address, name.

πρότερ-ος, -α, -ον, former.

πρόχειρ-ος, -ον, at hand.

πρύμν-η, -ης, ἡ, stern of a ship.

πρύμνηθεν, from the stern.

πρῶτα, *adv.,* first.

πρῶτον, *adv.,* first, in the first place.

πρῶτ-ος, -η, -ον, first.

πτέρ-υξ, -υγος, ἡ, wing.

πτοέω, *perf. pass.* ἐπτόημαι, terrify.

πυκάζω, cover thickly, deck.

πυκν-ός, -ή, -όν, close, thick, crowded.

πύλ-η, -ης, ἡ, gate.

πυνθάνομαι, ἐπυθόμην, learn, get to know.

πῦρ, πυρός, τό, fire.

πυρ-ά, -ᾶς, ἡ, funeral, pyre.

πύργ-ος, -ου, ὁ, tower.

πύργωμ-α, -ατος, τό, battlement.

πυρόω, burn.

πυρφορέω, be a torch-bearer, set on fire.

πω, yet.

πῶς, how?

P

ῥᾴδι-ος, -α, -ον, easy.

ῥέω, flow.

ῥήγνυμι, *aor. pass.* ἐρράγην, break.

ῥίπτω, throw, hurl.

ῥο-ή, -ῆς, ἡ, stream.

Σ

σάκ-ος, -ους, τό, shield.

σάλπ-ιγξ, -ιγγος, ἡ, trumpet.

σάρξ, σαρκός, ἡ, flesh.

σέβομαι *and* σέβω, revere, worship.

σεθεν, *as* σοῦ.

σέλ-ας, -αος, τό, brightness.

σεμν-ός, -ή, -όν, holy, august.

σθέν-ος, -ους, τό, strength.

σθένω, be strong.

σῑγάω, be silent.

σῑγ-ή, -ῆς, ἡ, silence.

Σκαμάνδρι-ος, -ον, of the Scamander.

Σκάμανδρ-ος, -ου, ὁ, Scamander, the river of Troy.

σκάφ-ος, -ους, τό, hull of a ship, ship.

σκέπτομαι, ἐσκεψάμην, examine, consider.

σκοπέω, examine, consider.

σκότι-ος, -α, -ον *and* σκότι-ος, -ον, dark. *See* 44, *note.*

σκύλευμ-α, -ατος, τό, plunder.

σκῦλ-α, -ων, τά, spoils, plunder.

σμῑκρός, *as* μῑκρός.

σός, σή, σόν, thy, your.

σοφ-ός, -ή, -όν, wise, clever.

σπαραγμ-ός, -οῦ, ὁ, a tearing.

σπάργαν-α, -ων, τά, swaddling clothes.

στέγ-η, -ης, ἡ, roof, shelter, house.

στείχω, walk, go.

στέλλω, make ready, send; *mid.*, set out.

στενάζω, groan, bewail.

στεφάν-η, -ης, ἡ, crown; 784, battlement.

στέφαν-ος, -ον, ὁ, crown (of victory), garland, glory, honour.

στεφανόω, crown, wreathe, honour.

στέφ-ος, -ους, τό, garland.

στέφω, put round, wreathe.

στιβ-άς, -άδος, ἡ, bed, mattress.

στολμ-ός, -οῦ, ὁ, equipment, raiment.

στόμ-α, -ατος, τό, mouth.

στράτευμ-α, -ατος, τό, campaign, army.

στρατηγέω, be general.

στρατηγ-ός, -οῦ, ὁ, general.

στρατηλάτ-ης, -ου, ὁ, general.

στρατι-ά, -ᾶς, ἡ, army.

στρατ-ός, -οῦ, ὁ, army.

στρέφω, ἔστρεψα, turn.

στυγέω, hate.

στυγν-ός, -ή, -όν, hateful.

συγ-γένει-α, -ας, ἡ, kin, kindred.

συγ-γεν-ής, -ές, kin, akin.

συγ-γιγνώσκω, *with dat.*, pardon.

συγ-γνώμ-η, -ης, ἡ, pardon.

σύ-ζυγ-ος, -ον, ὁ, yoke-fellow; 1001, brother.

σύμ-μαχ-ος, -ον, ὁ, ally.

συμ-πίπτω, *perf.* -πέπτωκα, fall with.

συμ-φορ-ά, -ᾶς, ἡ, misfortune.

σύν, *as* ξύν.

συν-εξ-αιρέω, -εῖλον, help in taking, removing.

συν-έρχομαι, come together.

συν-θέλω, consent.

συν-τίθημι, *aor. pass.* -ετέθην, compose, put together.

σύντομ-ος, -ον, cut short.

συ-στέλλω, enshroud.

σφαγ-ή, -ῆς, ἡ, slaughter, murder.

σφάγι-ον, -ον, τό, victim.

σφε, *pron.*, him, her, them.

σχεδόν, *adv.*, almost.

σχολ-ή, -ῆς, ἡ, leisure.

σῴζω, save, keep safe.

σῶμ-α, -ατος, τό, body.

σωτηρί-α, -ας, ἡ, safety, salvation.

σωφρονέω, perf. ἐσωφρόνηκα, be self-controlled.

σώφρ-ων, -ον, gen. -ονος, self-controlled, prudent.

T

τάλας, τάλαινα, τάλαν, wretched, unhappy.

ταμί-ᾱς, -ου, ὁ, steward.

ταπειν-ός, -ή, -όν, low, humble.

ταράσσω, trouble, throw into disorder.

τάσσω, perf. pass. τέταγμαι, order, command.

τάφ-ος, -ου, ὁ, tomb.

τάχα, quickly.

ταχέως, quickly.

τάχ-ος, -ους, τό, speed.

ταχύ-πους, -πουν, swift-footed.

ταχ-ύς, -εῖα, -ύ, swift.

τε, enclitic, and; τε ... καί, both ... and; also τε ... τε.

τείνω, ἔτεισα, repay; mid., punish.

τεῖχ-ος, -ους, τό, wall.

τέκν-ον, -ου, τό, child.

τέκ-ος, -ους, τό, as τέκνον.

τελαμ-ών, -ῶνος, ὁ, strap, bandage.

τελευτάω, finish.

τέρμ-α, -ατος, τό, end.

τέρψ-ις, -εως, ἡ, enjoyment, delight.

τετραβάμ-ων, -ον, gen. -ονος, four-footed.

τεῦχ-ος, -ους, τό, armour.

τῇδε, here.

τί, what? why?

τίθημι, θήσω, ἔθηκα, aor. mid. ἐθέμην, put, set up, bring about.

τίκτω, τέξω and τέξομαι, ἔτεκον, bear (a child), beget.

τῑμάω, honour, value.

τῑμι-ος, -α, -ον and τίμι-ος, -ον, valued, honoured.

τις, τι, enclitic pron., someone, something.

τίς, τί, interrog. pron., who? what?

τλήμ-ων, -ονος, ὁ, ἡ, enduring, wretched.

τοι, enclitic particle, indeed.

τοιγάρ, therefore.

τοι-οῦτος, -αύτη, -οῦτο and -οῦτον, such, of such a kind.

τόκ-ος, -ου, ὁ, offspring, son.

τοξεύω, shoot (with a bow), shoot at.

τόξ-ον, -ου, τό, bow; pl., bow and arrows.

τοσ-όσδε, -ήδε, -όνδε, so great. See 367, note.

τότε, then.

τραῦμ-α, -ατος, τό, wound.

τράχηλ-ος, -ου, ὁ, neck.

τρεῖς, τρία, three.

τρέμω, tremble.

τρέφω, rear, nourish.

τρέχω, ἔδραμον, run.

τρικῡμί-α, -ας, ἡ, great wave or swell.

τρισσ-ός, -ή, -όν, threefold.

τριτοβάμ-ων, -ον, gen. -ονος, forming a third foot.

Τροί-α, -ας, ἡ, Troy.

τρόπαι-ον, -ου, τό, trophy.

τρόπ-ος, -ου, ὁ, way, manner. See 1204, note.

τροφ-ή, -ῆς, ἡ, feeding, rearing.

τρυφ-ή, -ῆς, ἡ, delicacy, luxury.

Τρῳ-άς, -άδος, ἡ, fem. adj. and noun, Trojan, woman of Troy.

Τρῶ-ες, -ων, οἱ, Trojans.

Τρωικ-ός, -ή, -όν, Trojan.

τυγχάνω, τεύξομαι, ἔτυχον, with gen., hit upon, get.

τύμβ-ος, -ου, ὁ, tomb.

Τυνδαρ-ίς, -ίδος, ἡ, daughter of Tyndareus.

τυρανν-ίς, -ίδος, ἡ, kingly or absolute power, monarchy, kingdom.

τύρανν-ος, -ου, ὁ, king, ruler.

τύχ-η, -ης, ἡ, fortune, success.

Υ

ὑβρίζω, run riot, commit outrage.

ὕδ-ωρ, -ατος, τό, water.

υἱ-ός, -οῦ, ὁ, son.

ὑμέναι-ος, -ου, ὁ, wedding-song, wedding.

ὑμνέω, sing, sing of.

ὕμν-ος, -ου, ὁ, song.

ὑπαγκάλισμ-α, -ατος, τό, that which is embraced in the arms.

ὑπέρ, prep. with gen., on behalf of, instead of.

ὑπέρτατ-ος, -η, -ον, highest.

ὑπερ-τρέχω, -έδραμον, outrun, excel.

ὑπ-ισχνέομαι, -εσχόμην, promise.

ὕπν-ος, -ου, ὁ, sleep.

ὑπό, prep. with gen., by, at the hands of, because of; with dat., under.

ὕστερον, later, afterwards.

ὕστερ-ος, -α, -ον, later.

ὑφάπτω, kindle from beneath.

ὑψίπυργ-ος, -ον, high-towered.

ὑψόθεν, from above.

Φ

φαίνομαι, φανέομαι, ἐφάνην, appear.

φάος, as φῶς.

φάρ-αγξ, -αγγος, ἡ, ravine.

φείδομαι, with gen., spare.

φέρω, οἴσω, ἤνεγκα, carry, bring, bear, endure.

φεύγω, ἔφυγον, flee, escape.

φημί, φήσω, say.

φθάνω, act before or beforehand.

φθείρω, perf. pass. ἔφθαρμαι, destroy.

φθόν-ος, -ου, ὁ, envy.

φιλέω, love.

φίλημ-α, -ατος, τό, kiss.

φίλι-ος, -α, -ον, dear.

φίλ-ος, -ου, ὁ, friend.

φίλ-ος, -η, -ον, dear, friendly.

φίλτατος, superlative of φίλος.

φίλτρ-ον, -ου, τό, charm, spell.

φλέγω, burn, light up.

φλόγε-ος, -α, -ον, bright, burning.

φλόξ, φλογός, ἡ, flame.

φόβ-ος, -ου, ὁ, fear, dread.

φοίνι-ος, -α, -ον and φοίνι-ος, -ον, blood-red, murderous.

φόνι-ος, -ον, bloody, murderous.

φόν-ος, -ου, ὁ, murder, blood.

φρήν, φρενός, ἡ, mind; pl., wits, understanding.

φρίκ-η, -ης, ἡ, shudder.

φρονέω, be in one's right mind.

φροντίζω, fut. φροντιῶ, with acc. or gen., take thought for, pay heed to.

φροῦδ-ος, -η, -ον and φροῦδ-ος, -ον, gone, vanished.

Φρύγι-ος, -α, -ον and Φρύγι-ος, -ον, Trojan, Phrygian.

Φρύξ, Φρυγός, ὁ, Trojan.

φύσημ-α, -ατος, τό, blast.

φύσ-ις, -εως, ἡ, nature, character.

Φωκ-εύς, -έως, ὁ, Phocian.

φώς, φωτός, ὁ, man.

φῶς, φωτός, τό, light.

X

χαίρω, perf. part. pass. κεχαρμένος (with active meaning), rejoice. Imperative, χαῖρε, χαίρετε, farewell!

χάλαζ-α, -ης, ἡ, hail.

χαλκεομήστ-ωρ, -ορος, ὁ, well versed in arms.

χάλκε-ος, -α, -ον, of bronze.

χαλκόνωτ-ος, -ον, bronze-backed.

χαμαιπετ-ής, -ές, on the ground.

χαρ-ά, -ᾶς, ἡ, joy.

χάρ-ις, -ιτος, ἡ, delight, favour, gift of honour. See 781, note.

χείμαρρ-ος, -ον, winter-flowing.

χείρ, χειρός, ἡ, hand.

χειρόω, master, conquer.

χέω, pour, shed.

χήρ-α, -ας, ἡ, widow.

χθών, χθονός, ἡ, earth.

χλιδ-ή, -ῆς, ἡ, wantonness.

χοιρ-άς, -άδος, ἡ, rocky island.

χολόομαι, be angry.

χορεύω, dance.

χορ-ός, -οῦ, ὁ, dance, choir.

χράομαι, with acc. and dat., use, enjoy.

χρεών, τό, indecl., necessity.

χρή με, ἐχρῆν με, impers., I must, I have to.

χρῄζω, long for.

χρηστ-ός, -ή, -όν, useful, good.

χρόν-ος, -ου, ὁ, time.

χρῡσεοφάλαρ-ος, -ον, with golden ornaments.

χρῡσοκόμ-ας, -α, ὁ, golden-haired.

χρῡσ-ός, οῦ-, ὁ, gold.

χρώς, χρωτός and χροός, ὁ, body, flesh, skin.

χωρέω, go.

Ψ

ψεύδομαι, ἐψευσάμην, deceive.

ψῆφ-ος, -ου, ἡ, pebble, vote.

ψόγ-ος, -ου, ὁ, fault, blame.

ψυχ-ή, -ῆς, ἡ, life, soul, mind, thought.

Ω

ὦ, interj. of surprise, joy, pain, etc.; interj. with vocative.

ὧδε, thus.

ᾠδ-ή, -ῆς, ἡ, song.

ὠθέω, thrust, push.

ὠλέν-η, -ης, ἡ, arm.

ὤμοι, as ὦ.

ὡς, how (exclam. and indirect interrog.); in order that.

ὡσεί, as, as if.

ὥσπερ, as, as if.

ὥστε, with indic. or infin., with the result that, so as to.

PRINTED IN GREAT BRITAIN
BY ROBERT MACLEHOSE AND CO. LTD
THE UNIVERSITY PRESS, GLASGOW